SWIMMING
FOR ALL

David Sparkes
F.I.S.C., F.I.S.T.

Foreword by Rick Bailey
British Olympic Coach

Pelham Books, London

Swimming for All was
conceived and directed by
Imogen Bright,
21 Weedon Lane, Amersham, Bucks.

Designer: Anthony Lawrence
Illustrators: Peter Menim
Kate Simunek
Steve Wheldon
Cover photographs: Joe Dixon

First published in Great Britain by
Pelham Books Ltd., 44 Bedford Square,
London WC1B 3DP, 1985.

British Library Cataloguing in Publication Data

Sparkes, David
Swimming for all.
1. Swimming
I. Title
797.2'1   GV837

ISBN 0 7207 1611 X

Typeset by Burgess & Son (Abingdon) Ltd.
Printed and bound in Hong Kong by Mandarin Offset Ltd.

CONTENTS

FOREWORD

David Sparkes has tackled the very difficult task of presenting the theory and practice of swimming for swimmers of all ages, with skill and enthusiasm.

The clear narrative and the high quality of the drawings will enable the enthusiastic swimmer to follow the step by step development of each swimming stroke with ease. Whilst those interested in broadening a basic knowledge of the sport cannot fail to understand the teaching and coaching skills which David Sparkes neatly incorporates into the text.

This is not a highly technical book for the advanced teacher or coach, although many would do well to consolidate their experience by reading the relevant sections. I feel more certain that **Swimming for All** will take its place as a ready reference for participants of all ages involved in swimming for fun and fitness, and will fulfill the requirements of those involved in swimming club activities.

I am very conscious of the fact that to achieve the highest standards of performance and to represent Great Britain at Olympic level requires the best foundations in teaching and coaching in the early stages. David Sparkes has captured the essential ingredients necessary to provide everyone with a great start in the sport.

I hope the book will increase the reader's enjoyment in one of our most popular leisure activities.

Rick Bailey.
Great Britain Olympic Coach,
Los Angeles, 1984.

WHY SWIM?

Before beginning this book, it is important that the reader understands that we can all swim. Some of us may find it more difficult than others, but we are all capable of being swimmers. Naturally some people will become very good swimmers, while others will be barely adequate. But this is true of many things. While everyone can kick a football, there are very few who will become first division players.

Even if you do not normally enjoy taking part in sports, you will be able to get considerable enjoyment from swimming. Goals can be easily set and achieved. Swimming offers a wide range of skills and activity for everyone from the beginner to the recreational swimmer to the serious competitive swimmer. Although it helps if you are naturally athletic, particularly if you wish to become a competitive swimmer, this is not essential.

Almost all of us have experienced an initial fear of water. This is something which can be quickly overcome. Many of the skills described in this book are broken down into easy stages, and are intended to help you to gain confidence and to feel at home in the water. It is natural that you will approach your learning at the pool with some caution, but you will soon find that you are tackling it more boldly and vigorously.

There are many swimming pools available. There are also many clubs and groups where you can find teachers who will help you to perform the skills described in these pages. Swimming is an inexpensive sport. Little equipment, and therefore very little outlay, is required. Swimming also takes up very little time. It can be fitted into the routine of a business man or woman, particularly since some pools open very early in the morning and stay open late in the evenings.

If you are a family man with children, swimming enables you to enjoy an activity together as a family. It is one of the few sports which has a levelling ability, in that adults and children can play together quite happily in the water. What is more, there is no difficulty due to the difference in physical size.

Apart from the enjoyment to be gained from the sport, there are many reasons why we should learn to swim and be fully confident in the water.

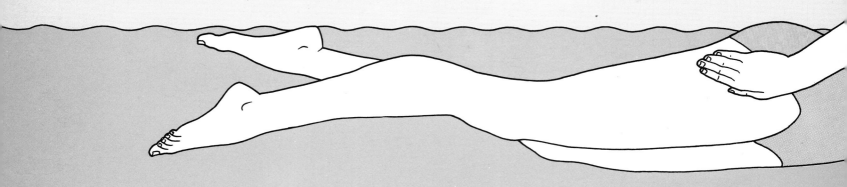

SAFETY

The most important reason for learning to swim is survival. With more and more leisure, much of our time is now spent on or near to water. Apart from yachting and canoeing, water sports such as windsurfing and waterskiing are becoming increasingly popular.

Without being efficient and happy in water, these sports are not open for us to try. When you go on holiday you will probably visit the seaside, whether in this country or abroad. You might find yourself near a lake or hire a boat. If you can swim, this will give your life an added dimension.

FITNESS

Exercise is an important ingredient of healthy living for people of all ages. Swimming is the perfect introduction to exercise, as the buoyancy in the water allows physical activity without too much stress. Swimming is virtually free of muscular injury, and is much safer than many other sports.

Swimming is a very good way of attaining overall fitness. It exercises more muscle groups than many other sports, and is particularly helpful for the heart and lungs. For these it can bring many benefits. It makes the heart larger so that it pumps more blood per beat. The effective area of the lungs becomes greater. The intercostal muscles between the ribs, and also the diaphram become stronger, making breathing more efficient. More oxygen gets into the blood stream. Dormant capilliaries in the muscles as well as more muscle fibres become effective.

Swimming is often used as a therapy for people who have suffered strokes or who have muscular problems. It is helpful at any age, and is rather like riding a bicycle; you do not forget how to do it. Even if you have not been swimming for many years, you will find that your old proficiency will return quite quickly.

COMPETITIONS

If you become a good swimmer, and you are a person who wishes to take part in a strong competitive sport, then swimming offers you plenty of opportunity. Competition is not restricted to swimming alone. There is competition in synchronized swimming, diving and water polo. However, you will need to be dedicated in order to enter a training programme. Today there are competitions for children from the age of eight upwards, and adults of any age can take part. There is a wide programme of swimming at all levels, from local clubs to international competitions.

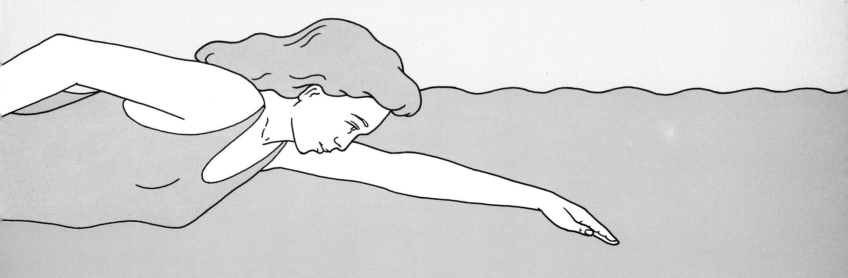

STARTING OFF

Without doubt, the most suitable place to learn to swim is in your local swimming pool. There are many hidden dangers in lakes, rivers or the sea, and you should wait until you are fully confident before you start swimming in open water.

You can find out the location of your local pool from the telephone directory or trade directories. Indoor pools are preferable to open air pools, where the water is not always kept at an adequate temperature.

DO I NEED A TEACHER?

Most pools offer some form of lessons, which may be helpful when starting off. Sometimes private individuals get together and organize their own classes, and often you will find classes for special groups. It is advisable to find a teacher who holds a full qualification from a national swimming organization. Not only will they have a good basic understanding of the skills of teaching swimming, but they will also ensure that safety precautions are observed. However, there are plenty of other experienced swimming teachers who can also offer helpful advice. So either talk to others who have taken lessons, or ask the staff at your pool.

Probably the best plan is to have the regular guidance of a teacher, for example once a week, to give you advice and encouragement. Then you can practice on your own and use the help given in this book for the rest of the week.

FEAR OF WATER

Many adults have a basic fear of water, similar to that of going to the dentist. It may be helpful to start by visiting the pool merely as a spectator in order to experience the pool environment, the smells, the noise and activity level. If possible, ask a friend, who is happy and competent in the water to accompany you, so that they can give you confidence and encouragement. This visit should be an enjoyable one, and need only last ten to fifteen minutes, enough to allow you to get used to the surroundings.

With some people, especially timid children, the problem of fear of the water can be solved by taking them to a swimming session, getting changed, and simply observing others playing. You can point out how much fun there is in swimming, and how the other children are enjoying themselves.

It is a good idea to find out when is a quiet time at the pool, and then to enter the water and start getting used to it without too many distractions around you.

Babies are sometimes upset by a noisy atmosphere. In these cases, it is better to attend mums and babies sessions. It is very important that neither mother nor father has any fear of the water. If necessary, they should conquer their own fears by visiting the pool and carrying out some of the confidence exercises suggested on pages 16–19, before bringing the baby or attending classes.

WHEN TO SWIM?

With modern indoor pools, swimming is an all-the-year round activity. There is no ideal time of day to go swimming, except that you should allow 45–60 minutes after eating a full meal, otherwise you could get cramp. Remember that schools and clubs often occupy the pool, which can very easily create a space problem.

It has been found that short regular visits to the pool on a daily basis produce the best results. After the initial learning period, frequent attendance will ensure that the skill develops and improves. A visit lasting 20 minutes is often sufficient. Provided the temperature of the pool is adequate, you can stay in the water for anything up to 45 minutes. But you should take care not to tire yourself. If you find that you tire easily, it is best to make your visits brief and frequent.

Learning to swim is a balance between maintaining good technique and improving your endurance capability. It is important in the early stages not to try to do too much. If you are tired, your swimming skills will suffer. However, you should aim to do a little more each time you go swimming, either by swimming a longer distance or by spending more time in the water. In this way, you will gradually improve your endurance capacity until you feel happy to remain in the water for prolonged periods of anything up to 45 minutes.

WHAT AGE?

You can learn to swim at any age. However, there are some points to note, depending on how old you are. Adults may find they have problems of flexibility, and that they are unable to endure prolonged periods of swimming. It is quite likely that you will not be flexible enough to achieve the stroke patterns described in this book, and so you will have to accept adaptations to these patterns. The guidance of an experienced teacher who can suggest adaptations to suit you individually would be very helpful here.

For many young children, the preliminary stages can be covered quite adequately during family visits to the pool. These should be as regular as possible, and should soon be combined with weekly lessons from a teacher, who will stimulate development and interest. Lessons from a teacher may need to be more frequent as the strokes improve, and as extra help is needed on the technical aspects.

It is generally thought that babies can enter an indoor swimming pool after the age of twelve weeks, provided the water temperature is around 83°F (28°C). Never take a baby to the pool while it has any infection. Since babies are developing continuously, there are special problems which can occur.

Parents should not expect too much too soon. They will need to accept that as the baby becomes more aware of its environment, it may not be as happy in the water as it seemed initially. This is quite natural. If you remember to treat the visits to the pool as an extension of play, the baby will develop water confidence quite easily. In any case, you must remember that a baby's head is heavier than the rest of the body. This means that it will float somewhat under the surface of the water, and parents will need to provide sufficient support. Eye contact must be maintained between mother and baby at all times. At the beginning, regular wetting of the head, either using a sponge or by splashing, will help to accustom the baby to the water. Take plenty of toys to the pool so that the visits become part of playtime.

As confidence grows, the baby will develop the skill of moving around the water happily away from the mother, who must however remain in constant attention. Make no attempt to introduce any water skills or stroke techniques. These are merely periods for establishing water confidence. In fact a child will not be ready to swim until it is between three and five years old, depending on growth.

Whatever age you are, it is good to play games in the water. Not only are they enjoyable, but they are an excellent way of acquiring water confidence. For some ideas, you should refer to the **Group Swimming** section of this book.

EQUIPMENT

Swimming is probably one of the cheapest sports to perform. You require only the simplest equipment. The list below covers all your basic needs.

Costumes Take care when you are selecting a costume. Do not buy one which is water-rententive or ill-fitting. After swimming, always rinse it thoroughly in fresh water and hang it up to dry. If you swim regularly, it may be desirable to have more than one costume, as it is not a good idea to put on a wet costume.

Towel A large towel is essential so that you can dry yourself properly after swimming to prevent skin irritations from developing. A second towel is a good idea for drying your hair.

Goggles are helpful for people whose eyes are affected by the gasses in pools treated with chlorine, or if you swim for long periods. The best goggles are fully adjustable so that they can be made to fit over your eyes and give an effective seal. When using goggles, safety must be observed, particularly when removing them. If you are not careful, they may slip in your wet hands, and because of the tight elastic used to retain them, fly back into your eye. Always grip them firmly and hold them clear of your face. While in the pool, leave goggles in position and avoid playing with them.

Soap and Shampoo If possible, wash well with soap before entering the water. Afterwards, have a good shower with soap, and shampoo the hair. This is desirable in order to remove all traces of the smell of chlorine.

Comb Dry your hair thoroughly before going out into the cooler air. You will need a comb, and probably small change if a dryer is fitted at the pool.

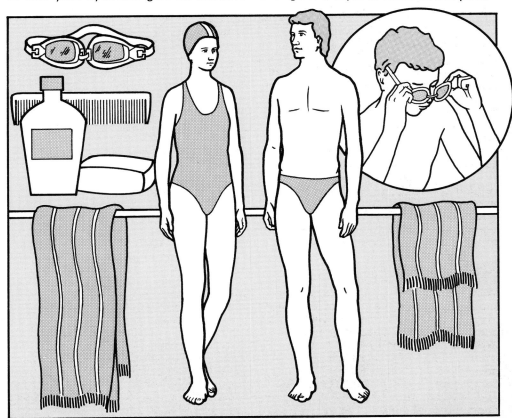

AT THE POOL

Whenever you visit the swimming pool, it is important that you follow a regular routine of cleansing, before and after swimming. This is to avoid the spread of infection, and it is obviously socially desirable that swimming pools should be kept as clean as possible. It also enables the pool manager to maintain the water with the highest degree of clarity.

When you arrive, especially if it is the first time, you must allow enough time to change into your swimming costume and to feel relaxed in a strange environment. After paying, make sure that you have enough small change available for lockers and hair dryers. Put away your clothes carefully, whether in a basket or locker, taking care not to soil your clothes with your outdoor shoes. It is probably best to leave your towel in the locker, as there are usually no facilities for leaving towels near the pool. Follow all storage instructions carefully.

Cleansing Before entering the water, you must be as clean as possible. Be sure to go first to the toilet, and to use your handkerchief. Then pass through the foot-bath and shower to give the whole of your body a thorough cleansing. If possible, use soap here, and if necessary, give your hair a good wash.

When you come out of the water, repeat the same cleansing procedure. Utilize the foot-bath and the shower using soap, and wash your hair. Again this prevents infection, and will remove the odour of the chlorine. Make sure that you do not cool off too fast. Go through the showers quickly, dry yourself thoroughly, and keep warm. Thorough drying is particularly important during the winter months to avoid possible problems from infection or chills. It is good to have two towels, one for your body and one for your hair.

Temperature The ideal water temperature is around 82°F (27°C), with the air temperature held one or two degrees higher. However, due to economic mea-

sures, some pools are now held at lower temperatures. If the temperature of your pool is not sufficiently high, you should reduce the length of time you stay in the water.

Water temperature is particularly important for young children, who need a temperature of around 85°F (29°C). The elderly too will experience considerable discomfort if the temperature falls below 80°F. For some disabled classes, temperatures as high as 88°F (31°C) are maintained.

AIDS

You will need one or two swimming aids, not only if you are learning to swim, but also in the development stages. Choose aids carefully, and make sure that they fit properly. You should also follow the manufacturer's recommendations for their use and aftercare, and check them regularly for faults. In any case, safety should be your main concern. If in doubt, ask the advice of an experienced teacher.

For the complete beginner, inflatable arm bands are probably the most popular aid, at whatever age. They provide good safe support, and enable you to experience the thrill of floating and moving around freely in the water. There are many different makes, but it is best to choose the double-chamber type, which provides additional safety protection, together with safety valves which you need to squeeze to blow up or let down. The most comfortable arm bands are those with a flat portion which fits underneath the arm.

In the early stages a very timid person may want to use arm bands together with a rubber ring to give additional support. As confidence develops, the ring may be discarded. Similarly, when you have learnt to swim, you may find it helpful to return to arm bands to help you develop further skills. Do not be afraid of returning to aids if they help to give you the necessary confidence for learning.

Solid arm bands look rather like discs, and have the advantage that you can vary the degree of buoyancy by the number of discs that you wear. The use of these is similar to that of inflatable arm bands, and they have the same wide range of application. Being solid, they are obviously safer than any form of inflatable support, which can always be punctured, but they tend to be rather less comfortable.

Inflatable rings, often known as rubber rings, are almost all made of plastic. They give good buoyancy and are useful both to the beginner and also when you are developing a stroke, as they provide support around the middle, which helps to keep the hips high in the water. As previously mentioned, these can be used together with arm bands. They can also be used with floats when practising. Once again, do not be afraid of returning to these if they help to give you confidence. Try to choose a ring which has a safety valve, and check regularly for leaks. With small children, rings can cause problems. If you choose one which is too large, the child may slip through it. With adults, the ring must always be large enough to allow full freedom of movement.

There are various proprietry buoyancy suits which have inbuilt pockets which are inflatable, or where you can insert buoyancy aids such as polystyrene strips. These suits are obviously safe if well fitted and the buoyancy aids are securely located. So make sure you select the correct size and that you fit the aids securely. Their advantage is that you can vary the degree of buoyancy, but always make sure that you keep them properly balanced, with the same amount of aids on each side. The suits can be used at any stage of development, but can be clumsy and unflattering.

Floats are an essential aid when you are developing the strokes. The most common one is the simple board. It is best to buy a board made of a closed cell material. Floats must withstand rough treatment, so avoid materials which absorb water or crumble. To begin with, you will only need a small board, about 9 × 11'' (22 × 28 cm). There are larger floats for sale, but these are intended for the competitive swimmer as a training aid for use once the strokes have been fully developed.

Pull buoys or leg floats are also useful in the development stages. They give support to the legs, helping you to maintain a relatively high body position and to concentrate on the arm action. The best ones are of solid construction. Other types are held together with string.

Flippers are not simply a fun device. They can also be a useful learning aid,

particularly in the development of the leg kick for butterfly, frontcrawl or backcrawl. The ideal flipper should fit well like a shoe, and you will need to renew flippers as you do a pair of shoes. If they are too big, you will have to work much harder. Adjustable flippers are cheapest, but not as effective as the more expensive shoe type.

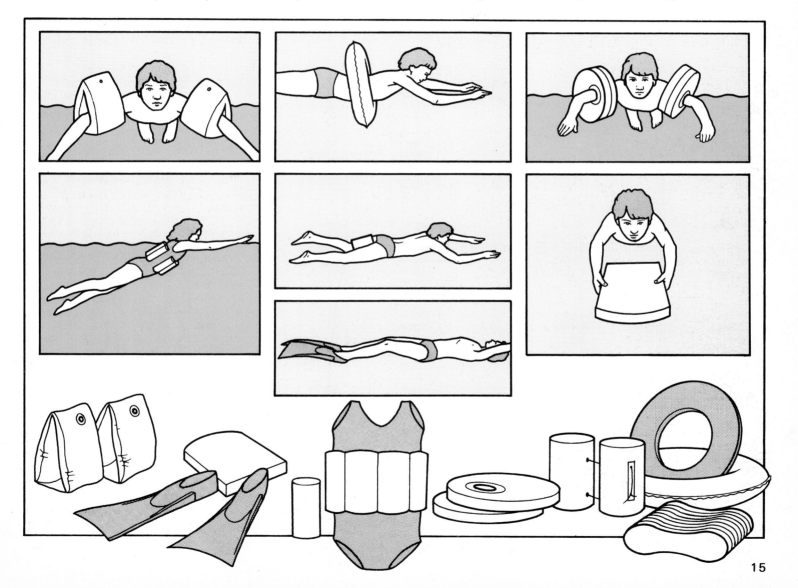

BASIC SKILLS

When you are learning to swim, it is a good idea to follow a logical sequence of basic confidence practices. If you do this, you will develop the correct water skills, and you will also build a sound foundation on which to base later stroke development in the future.

What follows is a step-by-step guide on how you can proceed. If you feel fairly confident, you may find some of the first practices too basic, and you can soon move on to the more difficult skills. However, you should not omit any of the practices, since they are aimed at developing certain aspects of swimming. You will find it useful to return to some of them in the future as a form of revision when you are learning more difficult skills.

MAKING A START

The First Step This is obviously getting into the water, and it is very simple. Having fitted your buoyancy aids (see page 14), enter by the steps in the shallow end. Go down backwards, holding the handrail firmly, and make sure that each foot is securely placed on the next rung before proceeding deeper.

Once you have entered the water, do not stand around with your shoulders out of the water. Acclimatize your body immediately with the water temperature by bending the knees and allowing the shoulders to submerge.

Bend knees and submerge shoulders.

You should then start to move slowly through the water away from the steps. Keep the knees bent and the shoulders submerged, and make for the bar. Try to get a feel for the water around your body, and use your hands to help you to move forwards. When you have taken hold of the bar, do not stand still. With your hands on the bar, start walking through the water. Once you feel acclimatized, you can change direction. Then you can speed up the process.

The First Kicks The next stage is to get your feet off the bottom of the pool. Standing in shoulder-depth water hold the bar from underneath with one hand, and place the other hand flat against the wall with the fingers pointing down. If you keep the shoulders low in the water, you will find that the legs move backwards. They will then want to rise to the surface behind you quite naturally. This is due to the buoyancy effect of the water.

Let the legs rise to the surface.

As soon as you feel that your legs want to leave the bottom, start to kick the water gently up and down. Kick from the hips, keeping the legs long and flexible, with the toes pointed. The action is similar to kicking a football.

Once you are happy doing this, you can increase the speed of kicking. Only do it for a short time. This is a very useful basic practice, and you can return to it from time to time to check your leg kick. But always make it brief.

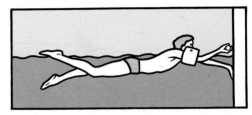

Kick from the hips, keeping toes pointed.

To extend this basic kicking, pull yourself along the bar, keeping the feet slightly off the bottom. This will help to develop the skill of moving through the water while also feeling the effect of kicking your feet. As you work on this practice, you will also experience some feeling of buoyancy and floatation. This is the next step.

Buoyancy Skills The easiest way to start floating is to float vertically, using the arm bands for support. Practice it in a depth of water just comfortable to stand in. Let go of the bar and put your hands and arms under water. Then draw your feet clear of the bottom by bending the knees. Keep your arms relaxed and imagine you are a shirt hanging on the clothesline, and your armbands are the pegs.

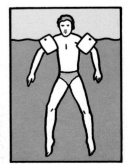

Start with a vertical float.

It is a good idea to stay close to the side so that you can reach the bar should you wish to put your feet down quickly. Once you feel confident, the next stage is to combine floatation and movement, in other words propulsion.

PROPULSION

In order to propel ourselves through the water, we need to use our legs and arms. The simplest arm movement is to use the hands as paddles. Press the water in the opposite direction to that in which you wish to travel. Practice paddling while you stand in the water, and try to experience the pressure of water on your hands. The simplest leg movement is similar to the action of riding a bicycle.

The first propulsion movements to attempt are similar to that of a spinning top. From the vertical float you can start to paddle with your hands and to cycle with your legs. You will find that your body starts to turn round. If you want to change direction, press the water in the

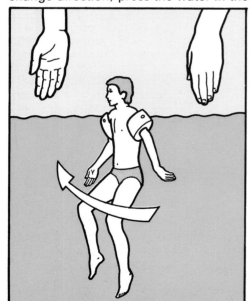

Cycle with legs and paddle with hands.

opposite direction with your hands. As your confidence grows, the speed of the spin can be increased along with swift changes in direction.

Movement Forwards is the next stage. Lean forward, place your chin firmly on the water, and extend your arms and hands forwards under water. You will find that your legs will rise to the surface behind you. Kick the legs in a similar action to riding a bicycle and at the same time push the hands forward alternately under the water and pull back, using them as paddles towards the chest. As you become more confident, this movement will become slow and quite precise. Try to reach forward as far as possible before dropping the hand to form a paddle.

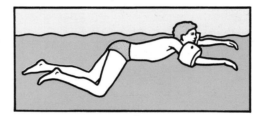

Legs cycle, hands paddle.

Movement Backwards Starting from the vertical float, tilt your head backwards until your eyes are looking up towards the sky (ceiling), and your head is cushioned on the water. Your legs will then leave the bottom. Paddle forwards towards your feet with your hands, in short movements, and cycle with your legs. You will find that you move backwards. As you become more confident, put your head further back until your ears are in the water, to bring your legs and hips closer to the surface.

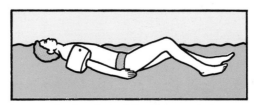

Legs cycle, hands paddle.

STANDING UP

This is a very useful exercise at this stage, and should be developed and practised thoroughly. It is particularly useful when someone bumps into you while you are swimming. You should never panic. Simply stop, regain your feet as described here, and then start swimming again.

To return to the standing position from the front, lift the head, tuck up your legs towards the seat, and pull the hands down and backwards. This will cause the body to rotate. When the legs are underneath the trunk, extend them towards the bottom of the pool until you are in the standing position.

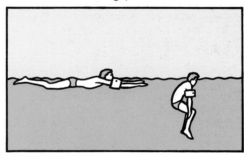

Regaining your feet from the front.

To return to the standing position from your back, lift the head clear of the water, tuck the legs up towards the seat, and pull the hands firmly backwards towards the seat. This will cause the legs to drop, and help the body to rotate. Press the feet backwards and down until you are vertical, and then in the standing position.

Regaining your feet from the back.

GAMES

There are many games you can play which help to develop your water skills so far. The simplest is to form a small group and to play copy the leader. Nominate a leader and then imitate all his actions.

You can also invent special circuits, for example spin six times, swim forwards one width, swim backwards one width, spin six times in the opposite direction, bob up and down twice in the water, etc.

OTHER FLOATS

You can extend your floating skills by trying out different positions. For instance, lean forward, put your chin on the water as though you were going to move forward. Put your hands out, just outside your shoulders to steady you, and let your legs rise to the surface.

Similarly to take up a position on your back, tilt your head back, look up towards the sky. Put your arms out to steady you, and allow your legs to rise towards the surface.

You can regain your feet in the ways described in the Standing Up paragraph on the previous page.

Starting a back float and a front float.

WATER BREATHING

It is essential that you wet your face at the earliest possible opportunity. Since you have to keep your face under water for at least part of all the swimming strokes, this is something you must get used to.

Start by simply cupping the hands and filling them with water while you stand in the pool, and go through a washing routine. This will accustom you to the feeling of having water over the face, and you can even practice it at home over the wash basin.

Then try putting your face into the pool. It is quite painless and easy. It may help initially to hold the bar standing in water of shoulder depth. Simply bend forwards and place your head in the water. Submerge the face only partially before you try full submersion. First up to your mouth, then up to the nose, and up to the eyes.

After submerging your face, you will probably feel like removing the water with your hands. Avoid this at all costs. If you shake your head vigorously, this will dislodge most of the water. In any case, go on putting your head into the water until you feel quite relaxed about it, and no longer feel the need to wipe your face with your hands. You can then go on to open your eyes while your head is under water. There is no pain associated with this, and you will find that your vision is quite good, although slightly blurred.

You must now learn to breathe in the water. This is the ability to breathe out (exhale) while the face is submerged, and to breathe in (inhale) while the face is above the water. Start with the following simple sequence: breathe in normally, put your head under water and open the eyes as described above, exhale into the water, lift your head out of the water to inhale, then return your head to the water, and so on. Eventually your aim will be to lift the head to inhale for the shortest possible time. Exhalation should be vigorous to ensure that all surplus water clears the mouth.

You are bound to swallow water from time to time. Even if it is a little painful and uncomfortable, this quickly passes. When you are swimming on your back underwater you may find water going up your nose. This can be prevented by breathing gently through your nose.

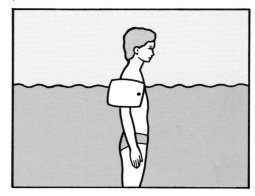

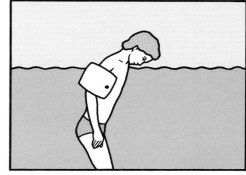

Simple breathing sequence for confidence.

Breathing Games To extend your breathing skills, two people can play at going under water and waving at each other. Another game is to select a partner. One partner submerges and holds up a number of fingers from one to ten. The other partner submerges about three feet away, opens his eyes and has to decide how many fingers his partner is holding up. Repeat until you get the right answer. Then change over.

Games: Counting fingers and waving.

MORE PROPULSION

In order to develop further your skills of propulsion or movement you will need a float. Hold the middle of the float out in front of you, with the arms extended and the face clear of the water. Instead of using a cycling action leg kick as previously, you should now try to kick vigorously up and down as you did in the first kicks at the bar. Keep your legs as long and flexible as possible, with the toes pointed.

As you kick, think about keeping a streamlined body position. This means you must keep the chin close to the surface and hold the hips high.

Next combine the kicking practice with the breathing sequence. Simply put your head into the water for short periods, exhale and then lift the head forward, keeping the chin on the water while you breathe in.

On your back, you can also develop from a cycling kick to the long and flexible up and down kick, which is similar to the basic backcrawl kick. Hold the float close to your chest, with the head well back. As confidence increases, you can grip the float less firmly, and eventually you can hold it over the thighs.

Kick with a streamlined body position.

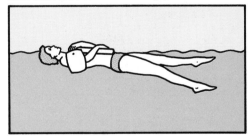

Develop a flexible up and down kick.

REDUCING THE AIDS

It is important to repeat these practices until you are both proficient and confident. You should then be ready to reduce the buoyancy provided by the aids. But proceed slowly, and do not be too ambitious. When you have developed further confidence, you must discard the aids altogether and attempt to swim a short distance without them.

Choose the swimming position with which you are happiest—your front or your back. At first it may be helpful for someone to stand beside you to give you some support to start with and to help you to regain your feet. Hands placed under the tummy and chest will help to establish a horizontal position. If you are on your back, hands held under the shoulders and the small of your back will ensure that your hips reach a high position.

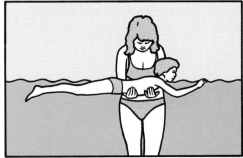

Support: hands under tummy and chest.

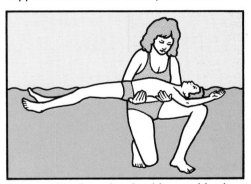

Support: hands under shoulders and back.

LEARNING THE STROKES

Do not do too much too quickly, but each time you go to the pool, try to swim a little further without aids. As soon as you can swim 5–11 yards (5–10 metres), you should start to think about learning to perform the correct strokes. Do this by studying the stroke sections of this book.

First of all, continue the stroke you have begun with, whether it is on your back or your front. You should concentrate more on the leg action in order to gain strength and to maintain a good body position. Once the leg kick has developed, you can move on to the arm action. Then as soon as possible try to begin the skill acquisition practices described for the other strokes as well.

UNDERSTANDING SWIMMING

Swimming is about the way you use your body, and how your body behaves in the water. When you take up the sport, and before you progress too far, you should think about the basics behind modern swimming techniques.

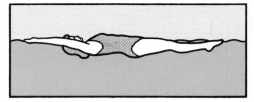

How a girl floats.

Although everyone is different, with varying degrees of flexibility, strength and natural skill, if you can understand how and why swimming works, you will find it easier to learn to swim well. You will be able to analyse your actions in the water, and to understand better the descriptions in this book. It will also enable you to make good effective movements, and eventually to gain maximum speed with minimum effort.

Let us consider first the nature of water itself. Despite being a liquid, water is extremely heavy, and anyone who has waded into a lake, a pond or even the sea will realize that considerable effort is required to move forward through the water as you go deeper. You have to use energy to propel yourself through it and to overcome the resistance to movement offered by the water.

The three basic ideas behind modern swimming techniques are buoyancy, resistance and propulsion. These ideas are all closely linked, and help to explain what swimming is about.

BUOYANCY

Why do some objects float while others sink? The answer is that it depends on how dense the objects are. If we consider a small ingot of metal, which we

throw into the water, we will observe that it sinks. However, if the same ingot is made into a can and sealed at both ends, it will float on the water. While the weight of the can and the weight of the ingot have not changed, it is the volume that has changed. In other words, the can is less dense than the ingot.

If we now compare the density of an object to the density of water, we see that if the object is denser than water it will sink, and if it is less dense than water, it will float. The closer the density of the object to that of water, the lower it will float in the water. That is why a piece of cork, which is much less dense than water, floats high, while an ice cube, which is almost as dense as water, floats low.

How cork and ice float.

How does this effect us? People are made up of many things—muscle, skin, bone, etc. All these parts of our body will sink. The only things that actually prevent us from sinking are adipose tissue (fat), and the air contained in our lungs. If we check the density of a human being, we find that it is very close to that of water. This means that while most of us can float,

the greater part of our body is submerged (see the drawing above).

How well we float depends on how we are made. For the girls, life is fairly easy, as they have a reasonable proportion of fat, particularly around the hips and upper legs. This means that they can float in a horizontal position quite well. On the other hand, men, who tend to be more muscular, particularly in the legs, find it difficult to float in anything other than the vertical position. Remember that young children, particularly babies, will float slightly submerged, due to the high relative weight of their head to their body.

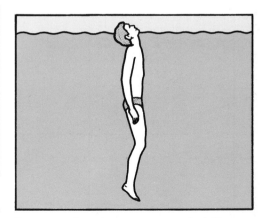

Some people only manage a vertical float.

A good way to test your buoyancy is to curl up into a ball, face down in the water, and to hold your legs in a mushroom float position. A buoyant person will float on the surface, while a person lacking buoyancy will tend to float a little below the surface.

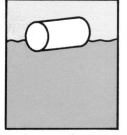

The difference between an ingot and a can.

A Mushroom Float in shoulder-depth water:

Submerge the head and flex the knees.

Curl up tight and grab knees.

Standing again.

To regain standing position, lift the head.

Those people who find that they are buoyant may be able to develop a flat horizontal floating position. Less buoyant people will find this position difficult, if not impossible to achieve. All this affects the way you swim. Very thin people may find it difficult to maintain a good position, particularly during backcrawl and frontcrawl. They will need to compensate by developing strong leg actions. For older people who have some fat, once they are confident, floating should be simple. This means that, in some cases, they do not need to develop such strong leg kicks, and can concentrate more on their arm actions.

As you will read later in the sections on the strokes, the head is the key to maintaining your body horizontal in the water. You can prove this for yourself. If you lift your head during frontcrawl your legs will sink. If you lower your head in the water, the legs will rise to the surface.

If the head is held high, the legs sink low.

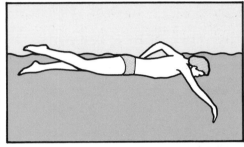

If the head is held low, the legs rise high.

If you can maintain a good horizontal body position, you will find it easier to move forward in the water, as you will meet less resistance, another basic idea in swimming, which we discuss on the next page.

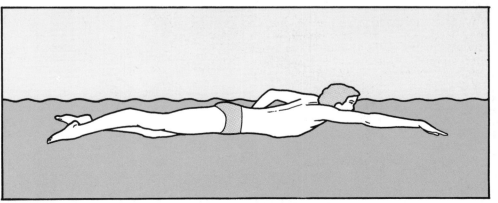

A good horizontal body position helps you to avoid resistance.

RESISTANCE

We have already observed that water tends to hold us back and to prevent us from moving forward, even when wading. When you are swimming, you should always aim to reduce resistance to this forward motion as much as possible. In this way, you will achieve maximum speed with minimum effort.

Let us consider two different shapes of similar size moving through the water. The first shape is a cylinder, and the second shape is a bullet. First of all, it will be obvious that the larger the shape, the greater the resistance to forward movement. This means that you should always be thinking about the size of your body in the water, and you must remember to keep your size as small and neat as possible.

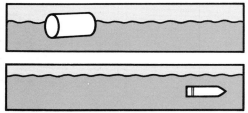

A cylinder and a bullet.

Second, the streamlined frontal shape of the bullet means that it can move through the water much more easily than the cylinder. The greater the frontal area presented to the water, the greater the resistance to movement forward. The golden rule when swimming is to minimize the frontal area, and to maintain good streamlining like the bullet.

Imagine you are trying to swim through a tube. You will thus avoid exaggerating your movements sideways or inclining your body. We have already discussed how raising the head tends to lower the feet. In frontcrawl, if you keep your head in the water, you

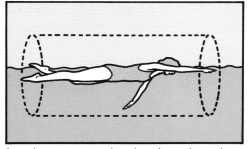

Imagine you are swimming through a tube.

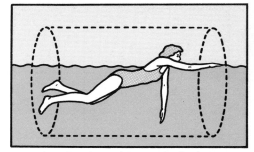

Keep hand actions close to the body.

will ensure that the legs and feet remain close to the surface. In backcrawl, if you keep the head steady you will prevent the legs from swinging from side to side.

The streamlined shape of the bullet means that water can move to the side and around it much more smoothly than in the case of the cylinder. The water swirling around the cylinder causes considerable turbulence in its wake. This turbulence is similar to what we see behind a boat. What happens is that the water fills in behind the boat in the hole which the boat has just left, and this swirling action tends to pull the boat back.

The different forms of resistance when swimming: surface, wave, resistance due to shape and the area presented to the water.

Turbulence: a boat and a swimmer.

The same happens with swimmers. In order to avoid leaving too much turbulence behind you, you must maintain a good streamlined body position. In breaststroke, for example, it is important to bring the heels up to the seat during the leg kick. But in order to maintain a smooth angle between the trunk and the upper leg, the knees must not be brought too far forward. Similarly during the arm action in breaststroke, you must ensure that the elbows are tucked in close to the trunk to avoid turbulence at the end of the propulsive phase.

Avoiding turbulence in breaststroke (1).

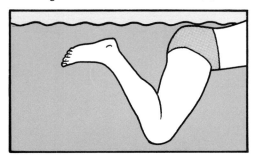

Avoiding turbulence in breaststroke (2).

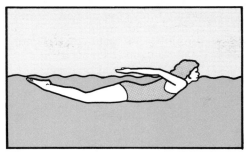

Butterfly: hips high, head low.

Butterfly: head high, legs low.

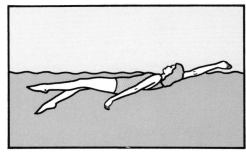

Backcrawl: shallow saucer shape to body.

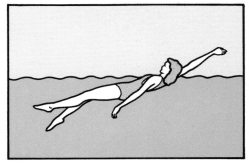

Backcrawl: head high, feet low.

Understanding Swimming

Resistance is also created by water clinging to the body, skin and swimming costume, and wishing to remain stationary. To avoid this, choose a smooth and well-fitting costume.

If you create excessive waves as you swim, you will waste energy and also create more resistance. If you maintain a good body position, you will avoid creating waves. Anyone will tell you that it is far easier to push and glide under water than on the surface. This is because you do not encounter any wave resistance when you are under water. This is a particularly important point if you are doing turns. If you push off from a turn under water instead of pushing off on the surface, you will travel faster and further.

INERTIA

This is another difficult scientific principle, but easy to understand for anyone who has ever tried to push start a car. It is very difficult to get the car to move initially, but once the car is rolling, it is then relatively easy to keep it moving, provided you are on a flat road. What made it difficult to start the car first was the inertia of the vehicle, and the need to accelerate it up to a rolling speed.

The same applies in swimming. If you maintain a constant and steady pace throughout, you will achieve a constant and steady rate of propulsion. But if you put on power intermittently, you will create a jerky stroke and less effective propulsion. If you can understand this, you will appreciate better the instructions in the frontcrawl and backcrawl sections about keeping the arm action and the leg kick continuous. With its constant propulsive force, frontcrawl will always be the fastest stroke, compared to butterfly or breaststroke, where power is only intermittently applied.

23

PROPULSION

When we swim, our means of propulsion are our arms and legs. How you use your arms and legs determines how effectively you propel yourself forward. This means that your constant aim while swimming should be to increase propulsion and its efficiency. You can see that in frontcrawl, backcrawl and butterfly, the main source of propulsion is the arm action, with the legs contributing only a little. However in breaststroke, the leg kick is an important feature, and contributes significantly to the propulsive effort.

It is now widely accepted that swimming strokes are a combination of a paddle and lift effect. Think of the simplest of the strokes, dog paddle. If you put your hand in the water and pull directly backwards, the hand is working like the paddle in a boat. Just as the paddle pulls back to make the boat go forward, so you press back in order to go forward. In other words, the body moves in the opposite direction to which you pull.

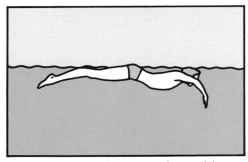

Butterfly: arms main source of propulsion.

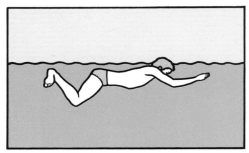

Breaststroke: legs main source of propulsion.

If we observe a cross-section of our hands and feet, we will see that the shape is similar to that of an aeroplane wing. The surface is curved on the top and flat at the base. The movement of air across an aeroplane wing creates lift, and it is this lift which generates propulsion. In the same way in swimming, it is the movement of the water across the hands and feet which creates lift, and in turn propulsion.

Many detailed studies of modern strokes have shown that a major force comes from this lift effect. The illustrations of the strong pulls of the frontcrawl hand action, show that the bulk of the movement is sideways, up or down, and that there is little movement directly backwards. We can thus conclude that the paddle effect in swimming is minimal.

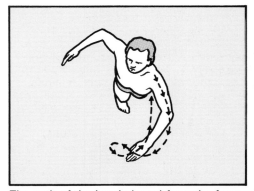

The path of the hand viewed from the front of an experienced frontcrawl swimmer.

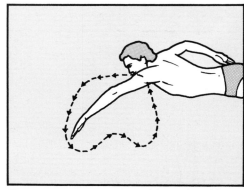

The same swimmer viewed from the side.

All the time you are swimming you are constantly changing the way you use your hands, and therefore their relation to the water. As you learn the strokes, you need to develop what is called a feel for the water, and to be aware of the way you are moving your hand through the water. If you can do

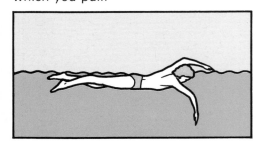

Frontcrawl: arms main source of propulsion

Backcrawl: arms main source of propulsion.

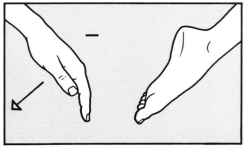

Hands and feet provide lift.

this, and follow the directions given in the strokes sections of this book, you will greatly improve propulsion.

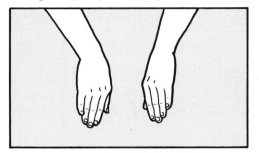

Breaststroke: hand pitched out initially.

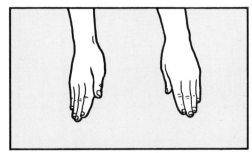

The hand pitch changes to inwards.

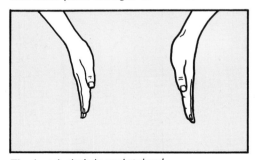

The hand pitch is maintained.

Let us look at frontcrawl again. It is important to secure a firm grip of the water when you reach the Catch position of the arm action, and to establish a strong down and out movement (Downsweep). This will help you to achieve the high elbow position necessary to maximize the pressure that you place on the water. The high elbow position will

The essential high elbow position.

also enable the strong muscles of the chest, back and shoulders to work effectively. It is helpful here to imagine climbing a rope. You cannot climb a rope with the arms extended, so you

need to get close to it and to allow the elbows to flex. This feeling of a high elbow is a feature common to all strokes, as you will note while reading this book.

It is impossible to gain a feel for the water without regular practice. The more often you practice, the more likely you are to develop this feel. The more natural this skill becomes, the more rapidly you will progress, and it is the particularly skilled performers who will eventually become proficient competitive swimmers.

To conclude this section, let us think again of frontcrawl, backcrawl and butterfly. In these strokes, the main source of *propulsion* is the arm action. The legs balance the arm action by maintaining a stable head position to give good (*buoyant*) streamlining and to minimize frontal area, thus reducing *resistance* to forward movement.

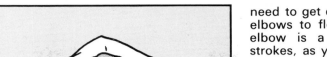

TRANSFER OF MOMENTUM

We have all observed this concept by watching snooker players. When a snooker ball hits another ball, the second moves off, leaving the first ball standing still. A good example of this in swimming is during the Wind-Up Start. When the vigorous circular movement of the arms stops, momentum is transferred to the body to maximize the speed with which you leave the starting block.

Sometimes transfer of momentum can cause problems. For example, in backcrawl. During the Recovery phase, if you stop the arm action as your hand enters the water, you will transfer the momentum of the Recovery action to your body. Your body will then drop beneath the surface in a rather bouncy manner thus destroying your good streamlined body position and increasing resistance to movement.

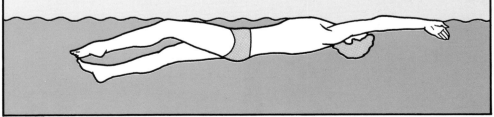

Backcrawl: transfer of momentum from the arm to the shoulder.

FRONTCRAWL

Frontcrawl is the most popular of all the swimming strokes. It is often the one which we learn to swim first, as the action is similar to walking, and is really only a development of dog paddle. When performed correctly it is certainly the fastest stroke, and was developed in its present form to meet the demands of competitive swimming.

In order to master the stroke, swimmers must observe two basic rules. First they must achieve good water breathing, and second they must maintain a good streamlined position. If you fail to learn good breathing, you will find it impossible to achieve a good body position. This makes it difficult to swim fast, and gives the appearance of an ugly unco-ordinated action, as well as being tiring. Good frontcrawl swimming should appear effortless and smooth.

BODY POSITION

The first golden rule is to maintain a good streamlined body position. The body should be as flat as possible in the

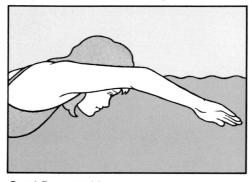

Good Entry position.

water, with the hips kept just below the surface. It will look as if the shoulders are high out of the water. This is because the shoulder of the pulling arm drops into the water at the same time as the shoulder of the recovering arm is lifted out of the water. The action is perfectly correct and natural, and should be encouraged. The leg kick will appear to just break the surface, causing a small splash.

In order to achieve this ideal position, it is best to place the head in the water with the eyes looking slightly forward through the water to a point 6" (15 cm) in depth about an arm's length in front. By keeping the hairline on the water level you will find that the correct body position is maintained. Depending on how buoyant you are, it may be necessary to adjust this head position. More buoyant swimmers need to lift their heads more, while more muscular swimmers put their heads deeper into the water.

Avoid any excessive movement of the head. If you move the head too much, it will look as if the whole body is waggling down the pool. Remember too that the more the head is raised

Ideal body position.

forward, the more the hips will drop. All this helps to create undue resistance to forward movement.

ARM ACTION

The arm action is the power house of the frontcrawl. It is important that it is both continuous and that the arms work alternately. We describe here the action of the right arm. When you have read this section once, you can read through it a second time, and imagine the same sequence for the left arm.

Entry The hand should enter the water as smoothly as possible. The movement should be comfortable and relaxed. The point of entry will vary from swimmer to swimmer, depending on how flexible you are. Ideally, it should be in line with the ear and slightly forward of the head. However, entry at any point between the centreline and the shoulder is perfectly acceptable. The fingers should enter first, with the elbow held high and

Shoulder rolls for maximum propulsion.

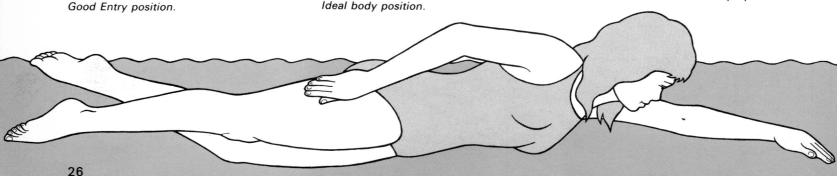

the hand pitched outwards at between 30°–40°.

Stretch As the right hand enters the water, the forearm follows through in a continuous movement to a comfortable stretch position. This action should be achieved without any movement up or down, simply following forwards through the natural line of the arm. Hold the hand forwards and relaxed. If the timing is correct, this extended position will be reached just as the opposite (the left) hand is finishing its propulsive phase of the stroke.

Catch As the left hand ceases to press the water, the right hand in the stretch position is flexed at the wrist and rotates to catch the water, ready to exert pressure out and back. At this early stage the elbow begins to flex, and the hand accelerates down and outwards.

Downsweep The next phase is a down and outwards sweep of the hands, with the elbow flexing and in a high position. Remember to pitch the hand outwards.

Insweep As the hand reaches its deepest point, it sweeps upwards and backwards from just outside the shoulder line to close to the centreline of the body. At this stage the hand is pitched inwards and upwards. Once again, remember to keep the elbow high. Flexion can be anything up to 90°. Swimmers differ here. Some do not reach the centreline with their hands, while others cross it. As long as these differences are not exaggerated, both are acceptable.

Upsweep As the right hand passes under the shoulder it should move into an Upsweep to press towards the hips. The hand now pitches out and up. Elbow flexion is reduced, but partly maintained until the hand releases the water close to the thigh.

Recovery The elbow will leave the water first, followed by the hand. The hand will be turned in towards the thigh. Make sure that the elbow goes high. This allows the hand to pass well clear of the water, and to swing forward in a semi-circular action, past the shoulder ready for Entry.

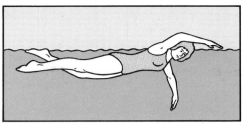

Entry.

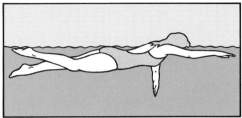

Stretch.

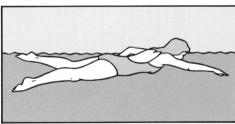

Catch.

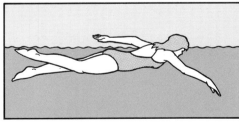

Downsweep.

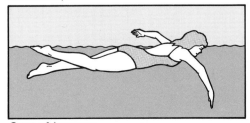

Start of Insweep.

Insweep.

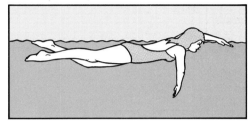

Start of Upsweep.

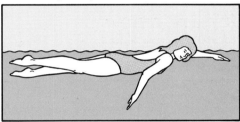

Upsweep.

Start of Recovery.

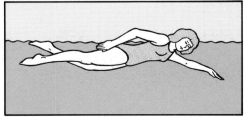

Recovery.

LEG KICK

The main purpose of the leg kick is to balance the movement of the arms and to help maintain the stable, straight body position which we have already described on the previous page. Make sure that the kick is continuous, and that the feet are extended during the kick, and if possible, slightly turned inwards. It is essential that the legs kick alternately up and down and that the legs remain close together. It helps if you have flexible ankles.

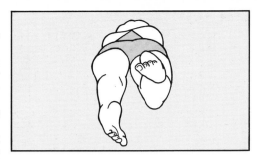

Intoed feet.

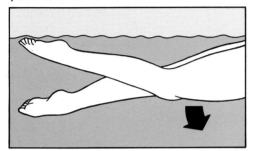

Upper leg initiates the kick.

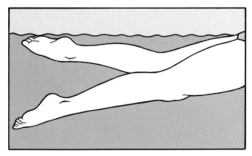

Lower leg drives down.

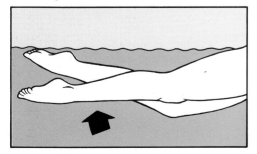

Upbeat strong but relaxed.

Make sure that the downbeat is effective. Start the movement at the hip, with the leg extended at the surface, and the ankle just below surface level. This causes the upper leg to drop, while the foot remains close to the surface, and leads to slight knee flexion. It will place the foot in a good position to gain maximum propulsion. Do not exaggerate the flexion. The lower leg should kick down, following the upper leg in a whip-like action. At the end of the downbeat, the leg is extended at a depth of 12–18″ (30–45 cm). The kick then changes to the upbeat without pause. Drive the leg to the surface without knee flexion, holding the foot in a relaxed position.

BREATHING

Breathing is a problem, because in order to maintain a streamlined body position, the face must remain in the water throughout the stroke. This can be overcome by taking advantage of the natural body roll. As the hand completes its propulsive phase and leaves the water for Recovery, the shoulder of the recovering arm rotates high out of the water. At this point you should allow the head to roll towards that same side, without lifting it.

In practice, it is only necessary to roll the head slightly to clear the water, since the swimmer creates a bow wave, which causes a slight depression in the water in line with the mouth. Never turn the head too far. Once the mouth is

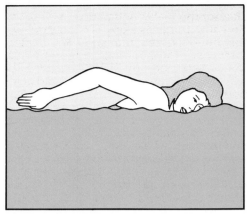

Head clears water surface as hand recovers.

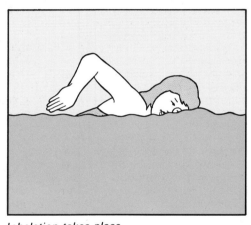

Inhalation takes place.

Head to normal position before hand enters.

clear of the water, inhalation can occur. You should have taken in enough air as the hand passes the shoulder during Recovery. The head can then return to the water before Entry of the hand. You will thus ensure a good streamlined body position for the beginning of the next propulsive phase of the arm.

There are two methods of breathing which can be used: trickle breathing and explosive breathing. Trickle breathing means that you exhale gradually into the water throughout the arm cycle, slowly clearing the lungs of air prior to the head clearing the water. Explosive breathing means that the breath is held until the head just clears the water, when exhalation is done explosively, with a strong blow out prior to immediate inhalation.

Supporters of trickle breathing argue that by gradually exhaling you prevent tension building up during the stroke, and you allow inhalation to occur naturally. On the other hand, exponents of explosive breathing argue that it provides a firm and strong chest base from which to work, and that inhalation is improved by a faster intake of breath. In fact, most proficient swimmers use a combination of the two, and it is desirable to practice both methods.

If you are swimming over a distance, it is advisable to breathe regularly. Do so once every stroke cycle. Some swimmers have a natural preference for breathing on one particular side. This should not necessarily be discouraged. For shorter distances, around 27 yards (25 metres), it may be possible to breathe every third arm stroke. This technique enables you to breathe on alternate sides, and ensures a good body position for longer periods. It improves performance by developing a more balanced stroke, and enables you to observe fellow competitors during a race. Unfortunately, this method can be tiring if you are swimming vigorously over a long distance. Once again, you should learn and practice both techniques.

TIMING

Frontcrawl is a continuous stroke, and the timing is normally built around a six-beat leg kick to each arm cycle. On this timing, the action is similar to that of walking. As the right hand enters the water, the left leg kicks down vigorously. Similarly, as the left hand enters the water, the right leg kicks down vigorously. It is not necessary to learn this timing technique, since it develops naturally as you master the stroke. But it is essential to ensure that a continuous leg kick is established.

Most swimmers need to develop a strong six-beat leg kick in order to maintain a good stable body position, and to avoid sideways movement. However, some swimmers can achieve this without kicking so often, and use variations. The major one is the two-beat kick. This involves one strong kick down from each leg during each arm cycle. Normally the downbeat begins during the Insweep phase of the arm action on that side, and is concluded at the end of the propulsive phase. When not kicking, the legs remain still, but must be close together to avoid creating excessive resistance.

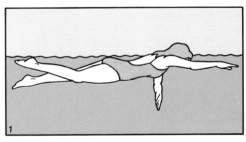

Left leg down, right arm enters.

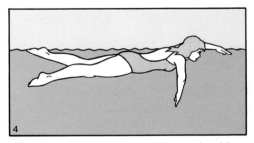

Right leg down, right hand below shoulder.

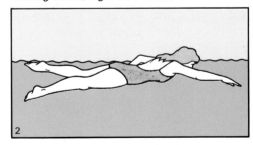

Right leg down, right arm Catch.

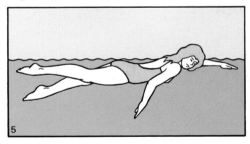

Left leg down, right arm Upsweep.

Left leg down, right arm Insweep.

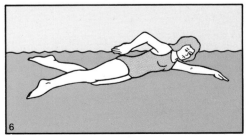

Right leg down, right hand recovers.

SKILL ACQUISITION

The swimmer starting from dog paddle stroke will have to overcome two problems in learning frontcrawl: holding the head clear of the water, and working the arms under water. Start by developing your water breathing in order to get the head into the water and to acquire a more streamlined body position. Exhalation under water should be encouraged as soon as possible. If you are unhappy about having water on your face or about putting your face under water, you should go back to the earliest water confidence exercises described in the **Basic Skills** section of this book.

Go back to the water confidence exercises.

Once you are confident about keeping your face in the water, you can start swimming with your head in the water. You can also use a float held at arm's length to strengthen and streamline the leg kick, and to develop a correct body position with the hips held high. Concentrate on kicking the legs with an extended foot and a vigorous action.

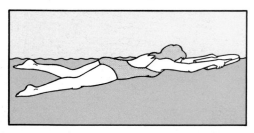

Swim with head in the water using a float.

To start developing the arm action, it is probably better to swim the whole stroke for short distances with the head in the water, simply concentrating on the working of the arms. Once the arm action has been developed, breathing can then be introduced into the stroke cycle. If this is difficult to start with, use a rubber ring to give additional buoyancy, or a float held between the upper legs may be useful.

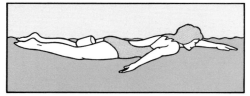

Arms only practice with pull buoy.

The skill of breathing and of blowing into the water as well as turning the head to the side to breathe in can be introduced when developing the leg kick in the early stages. Carry out the legs only practices with a float, keeping the face in the water, blowing out hard and turning to the side to breathe in. You will then find it relatively easy to fit this skill into the basic arm action.

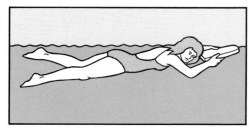

Legs only practice with breathing.

The co-ordination of the stroke, in terms of the arm action and leg kick, presents no real problem. This tends to develop quite naturally. But fitting in the breathing action can present difficulties. So concentrate on breathing out into the water so that you only have to lift the head clear of the surface in order to breathe in.

PRACTICES
Leg Kick

1. Hold two floats, one in each hand. These are intended to support the lower and upper arm, lean forward and kick.
2. Arms extended, hold one float forward, face clear of the water, practise the leg kick.
3. Arms extended, hold one float forward, face in the water, practise the leg kick, breathing out into the water, turning the head to the side to breathe in.
4. Arms extended forward, one hand on top of the other, head between arms, practise the leg kick.
5. One arm forward, one arm at the side, practise the leg kick lying on the side.

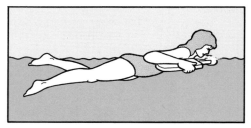

Leg Kick Practice no. 1.

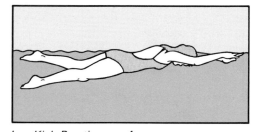

Leg Kick Practice no. 4.

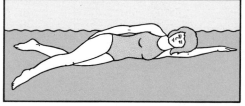

Leg Kick Practice no. 5.

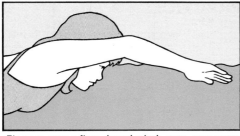 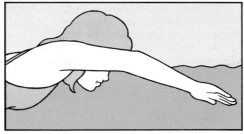 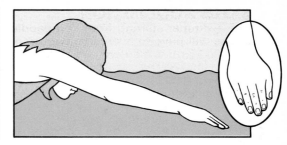

Fingers enter first, hand pitch out; arm extends to Catch; arm at Catch below the surface.

Arm Action

1. Swim full stroke without any breathing skill.
2. Swim using a rubber ring.
3. Swim using a pull buoy or float held between upper legs.
4. Swim full stroke gradually introducing breathing skill.

Breathing

1. Standing, submerging face under the water, blowing out, coming up and breathing in. Repeat many times.
2. Fetch objects from the bottom of the pool. Keep eyes open and breathe out.
3. During kicking practises, while using a float, develop exhalation into the water, turning to the side to breathe in.
4. Gradually develop breathing in full stroke swimming.

Frontcrawl arm action viewed from the front.

CHECK LIST

Body Position

1. Body flat and extended.
2. Eyes look forward through the water to a point 6" (15 cm) in depth about arm's length in front.
3. Water meets face at hairline.
4. Back and legs just below surface, not too steeply inclined.
5. Hips 1–2" (2.5–5 cm) below the surface.

Arm Action

1. Arm reaches forward of shoulders without stretching.
2. Fingers slide into water–no splash.
3. Order of arm entry into water: hand, wrist, forearm, elbow.
4. Propulsion starts with Catch, the firming of a slightly flexed wrist.
5. Wrist flexed and held firm.
6. Hand moves fast enough to generate propulsion.
7. Hand overtakes elbow.
8. Hand tracks elongated 'S' pattern.
9. Hand emerges from water close to the hip.
10. Arm lifted from water, elbow leading, fingers trailing.
11. Recovery clear of water.

Leg Action

1. Legs kick alternately and continuously.
2. Heels just break surface of water.
3. Legs extended, not rigid, ankles extended, toes point to rear.
4. Depth of kick about 12" (30 cm).
5. Kick starts from hip and travels down through leg to foot.

Breathing

1. Breathe regularly.
2. Breathing pattern fits stroke rate.
3. Inhalation takes place as arm commences Recovery.
4. Exhalation into water through mouth and nose.

Co-Ordination

1. Leg action balances arm action.
2. Tension creates rolling.
3. Leg rhythm can be 6-beat, 4-beat, 2-beat.
4. Stroke rhythm must be smooth and flowing.

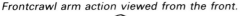

COMMON FAULTS

Body Position The main problem is the hips held too low due to incorrect head position, with the head held high out of the water. This usually means that the swimmer has not developed water breathing properly. You should return to basic confidence work, learning the skill of putting your face under the water so that you are quite happy to swim with the face submerged.

Novices tend to snap the head from side to side, until they appreciate the importance of a steady head position with the face in the water and using the natural roll of the body to breathe.

Arm Action All the faults associated with the arm action require detailed attention. They are usually due to misconceptions by the swimmer on how the action should occur. Ask someone to observe carefully what you are doing, and to explain each point, one at a time. Problems to look out for are over-reaching at Entry, with the hand entering across the centreline, which distorts the body position. Often Entry at this point is flat, causing excessive splash. Learn to 'spear' the water with the fingers.

In the early stages, it is common to try to pull far too deeply with a straight arm. Also swimmers tend to pull too quickly, with little or no power and without fixing firmly on the water. They

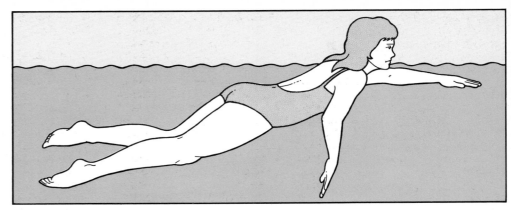
Pulling with a straight arm.

have the misconception that the quicker they pull, the faster they swim. Perseverance will ensure that you develop a feel for the water, and that power from the stroke comes quickly. Counting the strokes is a useful way of ensuring that you gain maximum propulsion from each arm pull.

Always make sure that Recovery is neither too rushed nor too slow, but fits in with the overall stroke rhythm. A frequent fault is for the arm to recover too high, with the hand well clear of the surface. You should try to avoid this, and concentrate on a high elbow Recovery, with the hand low over the water. This will help to ensure that a correct entry position is achieved.

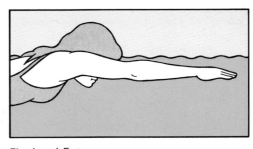
Flat hand Entry.

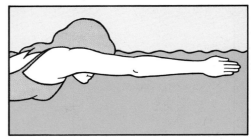
Incorrect hand Entry.

Hand over centreline during pull.

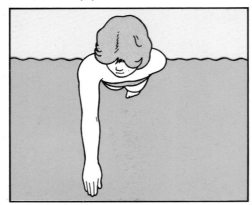
Poor body position: head held too high.

Arm Recovery too high.

32

Leg Kick Many faults develop in the early stages of the leg action. One is excessive bending of the knee, usually due to a misconception of the stroke action. This has to be corrected quickly. Carry out repeated kicking practices with emphasis on kicking from a 'long leg' and remember not to bend the knee, although some knee bend is essential for an effective kick.

A further common fault is that the foot is not extended. This can be due to inflexibility of the ankle, but very often is due to lack of understanding of how to perform the stroke. Swimmers who are inflexible in the ankle may have to do flexibility exercises to improve their range of movement. Most youngsters need only be encouraged to point their toes whilst kicking, to ensure that the correct foot position is maintained.

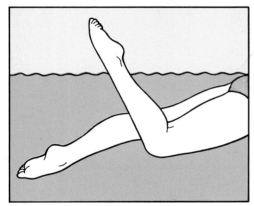

Excessive knee bend.

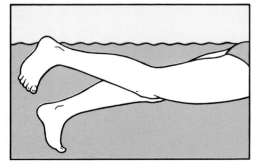

Inflexible ankles can be a problem.

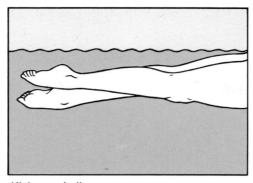

Kick too shallow.

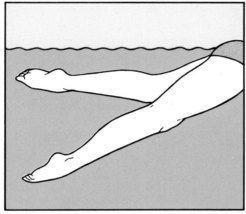

Kick too deep.

Other faults, include an inadequate kick. The kick may be too shallow or intermittent, or, indeed, too strong, with the foot coming clear of the water. All these cases are usually due to misconceptions by the swimmer. They can be corrected by repeated practices using a kickboard, with emphasis on a strong regular kick with the heels breaking the water surface.

Breathing Breathing problems are numerous and can be the cause of problems in other areas. Often the head is held far too high or too low. If the head is too high, the legs may be too low. If it is too low, the leg kick may break the surface of the water. So take care when observing problems to try to identify the cause. If the head position is incorrect, learn to adopt the correct head position, with the waterline breaking the forehead and the eyes looking down and slightly forward.

Swimmers often breathe at the wrong time during the arm action. This destroys the natural rhythm of the stroke. Correct this with repeated full stroke practice, concentrating on breathing at the right time.

Swimmers who hold their breath rather than exhale under water find that as the head turns to breathe, first they must exhale, then they must inhale. This means that the head is held clear of the water for too long, which causes timing and position problems. Learn from the earliest stage to blow out into the water, and only to breathe in as the head clears the water.

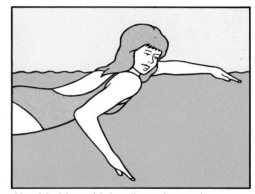

Head held too high, elbow dropped.

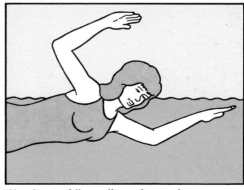

Head out of line, elbow dropped.

BACKCRAWL

In many ways the techniques employed in backcrawl are similar to those for frontcrawl. However, since you are swimming on your back, the problems of breathing are avoided. This means that you can maintain a stable body position, with the face clear of the water. As this is usually comfortable for the novice, the stroke should be learned at the earliest possible stage.

The qualities, which will be observed in a good backcrawler, are a strong, fluent stroke with no apparent pauses in the movement, and a stable head and body position.

BODY POSITION

As with all strokes, the head is the key to the correct body position. The ideal head position is with the ears resting just in the water, but with the head slightly raised. The eyes are looking up

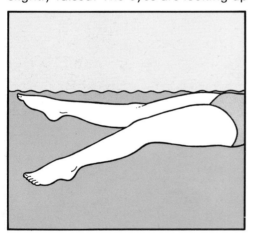

Feet kick to surface, toes pointed.

and backwards down the pool, as though the head is cushioned on a pillow. This ensures that the hips are maintained high and the feet do not break the surface of the water too much. The precise head position will vary somewhat, as it depends how buoyant you are.

The leg kick, which works continuously, should make the water appear to boil at the feet, with the toes just breaking the surface. The hips, meanwhile should always be stable, and a little below the surface, giving the overall appearance of a slight saucer shape to the body.

You should learn to roll during the stroke. Rolling is an essential part of backcrawl, and ensures that the correct hand movement is achieved during the propulsive phase. The degree of roll will vary from swimmer to swimmer, but normally it will be up to 45° in each direction.

The key points therefore are hips stable, just below the surface, and the feed just breaking the surface. Keep the head still throughout the stroke. If you roll the head, this will be transmitted into lateral movement of the trunk and legs.

Saucer shape to body.

ARM ACTION

The whole arm action must be continuous without pause, and as one hand starts its pull, the other hand should have just completed its propulsive phase.

Entry The swimmer should enter the water little finger first, with the palm facing outwards directly behind the shoulder of the entering arm, and the arm held straight. The movement should be smooth, with minimal splash and no flexion of the arm.

Catch The hand should now proceed smoothly in a down and outwards path to Catch. This should occur at a depth

Shoulder roll.

of 6–8" (15–20 cm) outside the shoulder line. At this point, flex the hand slightly to pitch down and out. Take a firm hold on the water to move smoothly into the first phase of the propulsive movement, the Downsweep.

Downsweep With the hand pitched down and out, the hand proceeds to sweep downwards and outwards in a circular movement. As this takes place, the shoulder rolls downwards. At the end of this Downsweep, the hand will be 18–24" (45–60 cm) below the surface and in line with the head. Then change the pitch of the hand for the next phase.

Upsweep The movement is now upwards and inwards as the elbow begins to flex, allowing the hand to move in towards the surface. Pitch the hand upwards and inwards, and increase elbow flexion up to 90°, until the hand is in line with the shoulder. At this point the hand should be 6–8" (15–20 cm) from the surface. If you have not rolled adequately, the hand may break the surface. This is a fault to avoid.

Second Downsweep Now gradually change the pitch of the hand to move into the Second Downsweep. With the hand pitched down and out, press back towards the thigh, finishing up close to the thigh with a strong press down towards the bottom of the pool, in a similar action to patting a ball. It is important to keep the pressure directed back towards the feet as long as possible before the final press down.

Release After the hand has pressed down and is just below the thighs, the hand releases the water. The shoulder is lifted out of the water by rolling, and is recovered with a straight arm in a relaxed manner. Rotate the hand with the palm facing the leg to lead with the thumb.

Recovery should be over the water in a vertical movement, with the arm remaining straight but relaxed. As the hand moves past the head, rotate the hand ready for Entry, with the little finger pointing towards the water surface.

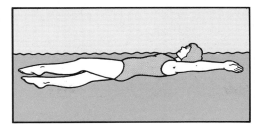

Entry.

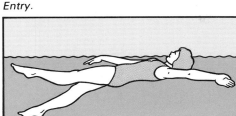

Catch.

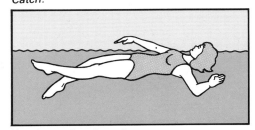

Hand transfers from Downsweep to Insweep.

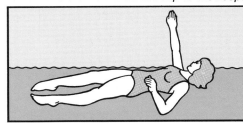

Start of Second Downsweep.

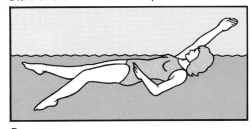

Downsweep.

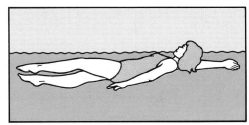

Downsweep complete.

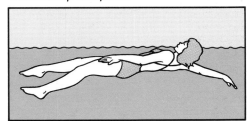

Release.

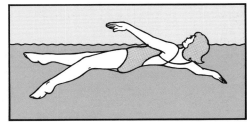

Recovery starts.

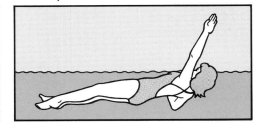

Hand rotates for Entry.

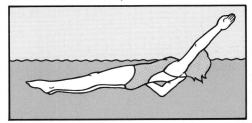

Hand about to enter water.

LEG KICK

The legs should operate alternately in close proximity to one another. They play an important part in ensuring that a stable body position is maintained throughout the stroke. They also help the swimmer to swim in a straight line. The leg kick is similar in style to that of frontcrawl, since it is continuous and uses an extended foot position.

It is important to concentrate on initiating a strong upbeat from the hips.

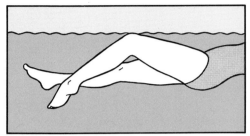

Strong upbeat with legs.

This is a similar action to kicking a football. Whilst knee bend is essential for an effective kick, this should not be exaggerated. At no point should the knee break the surface of the water.

Start with the leg near to the surface. Drop the leg without flexion of the knee, with the foot held in a normal relaxed position. As the leg reaches a point 15–18″ (37–45 cm) below the surface, the upper leg begins to rise. The lower leg continues to fall slightly, causing a little flexion of the knee. At

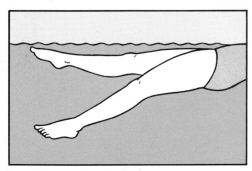

Drop the leg without flexion.

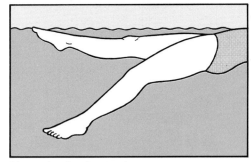

Upper leg begins to rise.

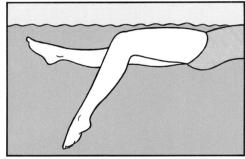

Increase flexion at the knee.

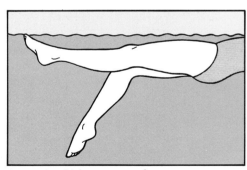

Lower leg kicks up to surface.

this point the foot must be in an extended position, if possible slightly in-toed, ready to press against the water. As the upper leg continues to rise, you should increase flexion at the knee until the lower leg begins to rise upwards. The lower leg then kicks upwards vigorously in a whip-like action, catching up with the upper leg as the toe breaks the surface.

BREATHING

Although breathing presents no significant problems, since the face remains clear of the water throughout the stroke, it is important to concentrate on breathing regularly and deliberately. A good technique is to breathe out as one arm recovers, and to breathe in as the other arm recovers. This usually establishes a regular pattern, and assists in the development of a smooth, continuous stroke.

The novice may move his head from side to side with the arm movements. This will lead to snaking, and should be corrected by developing a steady head position. Also some discomfort may be experienced by swimmers with water washing over their face. This will discourage regular breathing, and can be corrected by lifting the head slightly further forward.

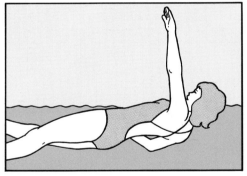

Breathe out as one arm recovers.

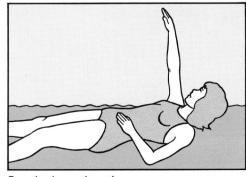

Breathe in as the other arm recovers.

TIMING

The basic timing is similar to that of frontcrawl, and again can be compared to walking. The main point to be borne in mind is that it is a continuous stroke with no pause at all. The arm action must be matched with the six-beat leg kick. Unlike frontcrawl, there are no variations to this basic timing. This is because the six-beat leg kick is essential to ensure that a good body position is maintained, and also to balance with the arm action. If you fail to establish this continuous leg kick, you will have strong sideways movements of the legs as you swim, and you will appear to snake down the pool.

The timing is as follows. As the right arm enters the water, the left leg kicks up vertically. Similarly, as the left arm enters the water, the right leg kicks up vigorously. Swimmers do not need to be taught this timing, since it comes quite naturally as you become more proficient in the stroke.

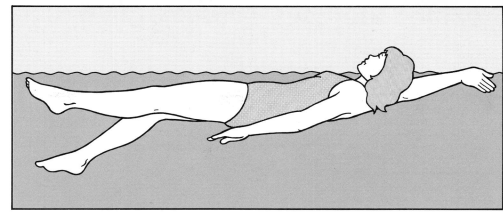

The right hand enters the water as the left leg kicks up.

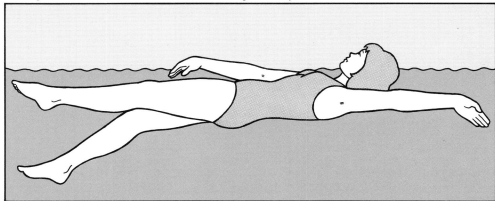

The right arm finishes propulsion when the left arm is at Catch.

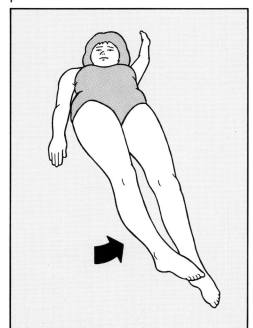

Bad leg kicks lead to sideways movement.

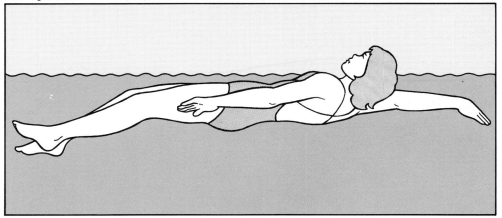

The left arm rises to Recovery as the right arm presses to Catch.

SKILL AQUISITION

You can start swimming on the back at the earliest possible stage. Be sure that you have overcome your initial fears about lying back on the water by returning once again to the water confidence exercises described in the **Basic Skills** section of this book. A rubber ring or float may be used to begin with for extra support, and to ensure that a good body position is achieved.

Concentrate first, as with frontcrawl, on developing an effective leg kick by working with a float. Make sure that the leg kick is continuous, and that an extended foot position is maintained. This will be much easier if you hold your head in the correct position, with the ears just resting in the water.

Once a reasonable leg kick has been achieved, you can then begin to develop a strong effective arm action. This can probably be best practised using the full stroke. You may need the additional support of a rubber ring here until confidence has been fully gained.

In the early phases of developing the arm action, many swimmers prefer to start with a basic straight arm pull, entering the water a little wide of the shoulder, and pulling round in a shallow semi-circular action with a straight arm. If you do this, remember that it is important to keep the pull shallow, and that the action is continuous and without pause. As soon as some competence has been achieved, you should then begin to develop the more effective bent arm pull. However, if you can start with some form of bent arm action, this will simplify the learning process.

The development of timing requires little attention, as this tends to come naturally. It is only necessary to ensure that the leg kick is continuous and that the arm action occurs without pause.

Do not forget the breathing. The novice swimmer sometimes tends to hold his breath for too long, so remember to breathe regularly. A useful tip is to breathe out as one arm recovers, and in as the other arm recovers.

PRACTICES
Leg Kick

1. Hold two floats under the forearm and upper arm, lie back on the water and practise the leg kick.
2. Hold one float on the chest with both hands, practise the leg kick.
3. Hold one float with both hands across the upper part of the legs, practise the leg kick checking that the legs do not break the surface.
4. Practise the leg action whilst hand-sculling beside the hips.
5. Practise the leg action with no assistance from the hands.

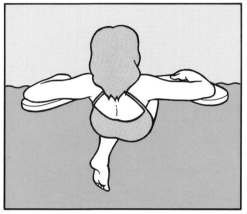

Leg Practice no. 1.

Straight arm pull with little shoulder roll.

Bent arm pull with more shoulder roll.

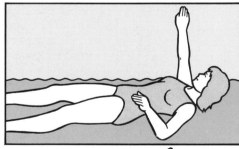

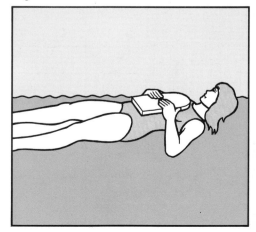

Leg Practice no 2.

6. Practise the leg kick with arms extended beyond the head, hands together.

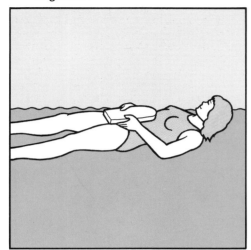

Leg Practice no. 3.

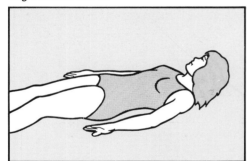

Leg Practice no. 4.

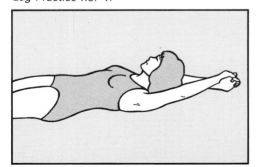

Leg Practice no. 6.

Arm Action
1. Practise the arm action using a partially inflated rubber ring.
2. Hold float under one arm, whilst using other arm, together with a strong leg kick.
3. Hand-scull whilst kicking. When body position established, introduce arm action.
4. Swim the full stroke, concentrating on correct arm action

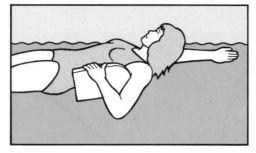

Arm Practice no. 2.

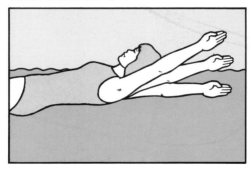

Order of arm Entry.

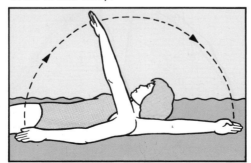

The way the hand changes pitch.

CHECK LIST

Body Position
1. Body horizontal, extended and almost flat.
2. Chest and head level with the water.
3. Hips beneath the water
4. Angle of head slightly forward.
5. Rolling of shoulders acceptable.
6. Hold head steady.
7. Body remains straight.

Arm Action
1. Straight arm reaches behind shoulder at Entry.
2. Arm entry must be controlled.
3. Order of arm entry into water: elbow, forearm, hand.
4. Recovery takes place above water.
5. Propulsive phase commences with Catch.
6. Elbow bends as hand is pulled.
7. Propulsive phase traces an elongated 'S' pattern.
8. Propulsion finishes level with waist.
9. Hand presses down at end of propulsion.
10. Hand leaves water in vertical line.
11. On Recovery arm fully extended, elbow straight, wrist relaxed.

Leg Kick
1. Legs extended, toes pointed.
2. Feet pointed and intoed for upbeat.
3. Hold legs close together.
4. Legs kick alternately.
5. Leg action starts from hip.
6. Relax ankles on downbeat.
7. At end of downbeat, leg slightly bent at knee.
8. Legs straighten on upbeat in whip-like action.
9. Toes break surface on upbeat.

Co-Ordination
1. Leg action balances rolling arm action.
2. Six-beat rapid kicking of legs.
3. No problems with breathing.

COMMON FAULTS

Body Position For effective backstroke swimming it is essential to maintain a good body position. The main faults usually stem from an incorrect head position. Either the head is held too high, causing the feet to be too low, or there is excessive movement of the head from side to side, which results in a vigorous swinging action of the legs. Some novice swimmers, in an attempt

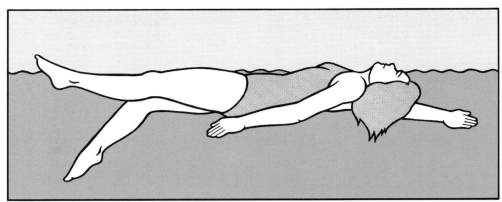

Head too far back, feet above water.

Head too high, legs too low.

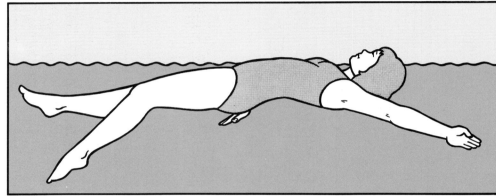

Arched back, chest too high.

Excessive head movement.

these points should be avoided by to ensure that the legs come up to the surface of the water, will in fact push the head back too far into the pool. All

ensuring that the head is held in the correct position in the water with the ears just submerged. Remember also to hold the head steady throughout the stroke.

Excessive arching of the back should also be avoided, as this is unnecessary. Provided the leg kick is strong and just breaking the surface of the water, the correct body position should be achieved as long as the head is held in the correct position.

Arm Action As we have already discussed on page 24 the arms are the 'power house' of backcrawl and it is important that a precise arm action is followed. Many of the faults associated with it are due to lack of precision in the

movements. For example, Entry over the centre line or wide of the shoulder rather than directly in line with the shoulder, pulling too deeply and recovering over the centreline of the body, can all lead to problems.

Entry over centreline.

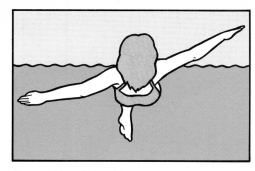

Entry wide of shoulder.

Pull too deep.

Recovery over centreline.

Swimmers should learn to carry out the arm movements as carefully as possible from the earliest stages. With the novice, pauses during the arm action are often evident, and so a continuous action should be encouraged at all times. Once you develop a bent arm pull, remember to maintain a high elbow position throughout the stroke. It is very common to drop the elbow during backcrawl, and this leads to a loss of power.

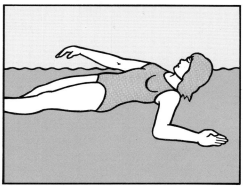

Dropped elbow.

Leg Kick Many of the faults associated with the frontcrawl leg kick can be referred to in backcrawl. For example, there is kicking without the foot properly extended, kicking unevenly, or not kicking continuously. To correct these, you should probably return to the

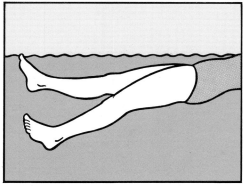

Foot not extended.

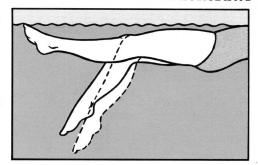

Kicking unevenly.

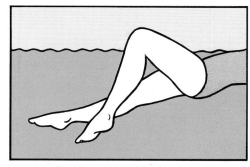

Cycling legs instead of kicking from hips.

basic kicking practices. Concentrate on maintaining an extended foot, and make sure that the kick is continuous and strong.

A particular problem with backstrokers, however, is that they tend to cycle the legs rather than kick from the hips. This fault can be recognized by the knees breaking the surface of the water throughout the stroke. It should be corrected by returning to the practice of holding the float over the thighs, while you concentrate on maintaining a leg kick beneath the water surface and kicking with a long leg.

Breathing The major breathing fault is not breathing regularly. Learn to breathe out as one arm recovers and to breathe in as the other arm recovers in order to avoid this problem. Also, if you take care to ensure that the head is in the correct position, you will avoid discomfort with water running over the face.

BREASTSTROKE

Breaststroke is the oldest of the swimming strokes, and can be compared to the action of a frog swimming. Some people find that a circular movement of the legs comes naturally, and so learn to swim by this method. The stroke is popular with recreational swimmers, as it is fairly easy to keep the face above the water. This allows you to breathe easily and to observe where you are going, which is desirable when swimming in a busy pool.

Unfortunately, if you do hold your head high out of the water, you will tend to drop the hips, and thus fail to achieve a good body position. Even if you just swim for recreation, you should try to improve the stroke by developing the skills described in this section. On the other hand, competitive breaststroke swimmers must comply with certain strict rules.

Breaststroke depends more than any other on a strong and effective leg kick. The arms and legs must each move simultaneously. Timing is critical, with the arm action occurring first, followed by the strong leg kick.

BODY POSITION

The key to an effective body position lies with the head and the hips being held as high as possible. To comply with swimming law, the head must remain above the surface throughout the stroke, and the body must remain perfectly level on the breast.

Some swimmers manage to maintain a flat body position throughout, and breathe by simply extending the neck. However modern techniques develop a powerful accelerating arm action with a strong final propulsive phase. These cause the swimmer to

naturally rise high out of the water towards the end of the pull without letting the hips drop too much. If you have a flexible spine, this will help to maintain a high hip position. As the arms go forward for Extension, the head goes back into the water until the water breaks the hairline. Make sure that the head does not submerge at this point.

ARM ACTION

Start with the arms in the extended and stretched position, making sure that the hands are correctly aligned for the initial movement. The palms should be facing outwards, the thumb and first finger touching, and the hands and wrists tilted slightly so that the little finger is somewhat higher in the water than the thumbs. The hands are thus in a strong position to begin the first movement. They should be about 6'' (15 cm) below the surface. Keep the arms straight so that you ensure that

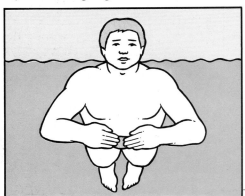

Head lifts to breathe.

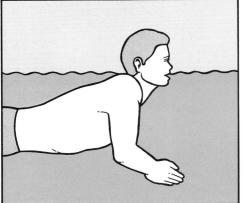

Head lifts to breathe.

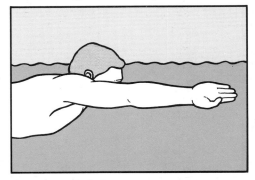

Arms extended, face returns to water.

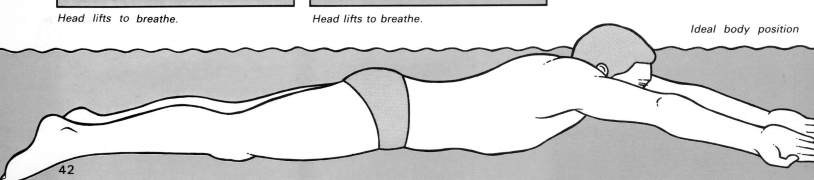

Ideal body position

42

the shoulders are streamlined.

Outsweep This is simply a movement of the hands outwards, without any flexion of the arms, until the arms are just outside the shoulder width ready for Catch. During this movement, the pitch of the hands should be kept in an outwards and backwards line.

Catch occurs just outside the shoulder width. You should change the pitch of the hand from outwards and backwards to an outwards, backwards and downwards movement, ready for the Downsweep phase.

Downsweep is a strong accelerating movement in a downwards and outwards circular path during which the elbows should flex. Keep the elbows high during this movement to ensure the correct path of the hands. The pitch of the hands should be downwards, backwards and outwards.

Insweep A smooth transition from Downsweep to Insweep occurs at the deepest point in the arm pull. This is a circular action, with the hands pressing inwards, and beginning to move upwards and backwards. Change the pitch of the hands gradually to inwards and upwards, but in an accelerating manner. The elbows follow the hands through, also in an inwards action. To maintain good streamlining, make sure that the hands lead the elbows throughout. When this movement is complete, the elbows should be close to the ribs, with the hands together just in front of the shoulders.

Extension The arms must now extend forward to the stretch position. If you find your palms facing upwards at this stage, you must gradually rotate them to the correct hand position as you extend your arms. The thumb and first finger should be touching, with the little finger high, as described at the beginning of this section.

As with the leg action, there is no pause here. But you must always reach this position before proceeding to the Outsweep. Novices may pause briefly so that the correct leg action timing takes place.

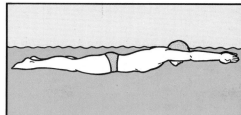
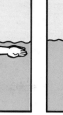

Extension.

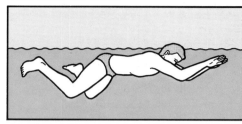

Feet catch the water.

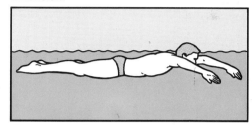

Outsweep to Catch.

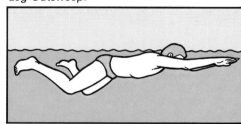

Leg Outsweep.

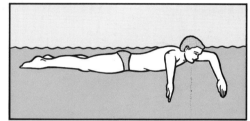

Downsweep.

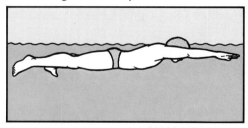

Start of leg Downsweep.

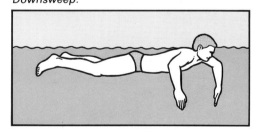

Insweep.

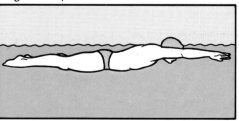

Leg Insweep.

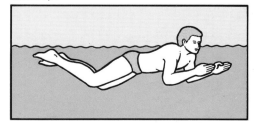

Hands and legs recover.

Legs at Extension.

LEG KICK

Unlike the other strokes, a major contribution to propulsion is made by the leg kick. Also the foot position, often difficult to start with, is different in that a flat foot (dorsi-flexed) is necessary for propulsion.

Extension Start with the legs extended. The feet should be together with the toes pointed in a streamlined position. From here the legs recover smoothly.

Recovery Begin to bend the knees, enabling the feet to move up towards the seat. Concentrate on drawing up your feet without allowing the knees to recover forward, and maintain an angle of 130°–140° between the trunk and upper leg. Keep the feet close together until the completion of the action, when they will separate to hip width apart above the knees. The feet should finish as close to the seat as possible, but this will depend on how flexible you are.

Outsweep Before the strong Outsweep kick can occur, the feet must be placed in the correct position for the kick. Cock the feet by drawing them up into a flat position, with the toes pointed outwards in an east-west action, and the soles of the feet facing backwards. At this stage, the feet will be a little outside the hips, and ready to begin the strong outwards movement. This is a circular outwards movement, with the knees extending. The legs then begin to move together slightly into the Downsweep.

Downsweep It is important to hold the feet in a cocked position throughout. Movement continues in a rounded action downwards and inwards, until the legs are straight. It is completed by a strong accelerating Insweep.

Insweep The feet now change pitch gradually to a pointed position. Keep the action continuous and accelerating. On completion, the legs should be extended and close together to begin Recovery, as described at the start of this section. As with the arm action, there is no pause here. Always make sure that the feet complete the movement.

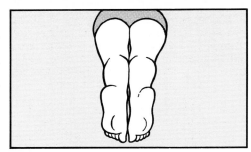

Extension.

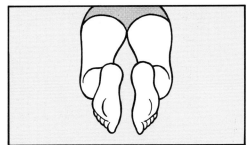

Recovery starts.

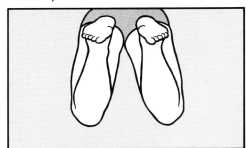

Heels recover to seat.

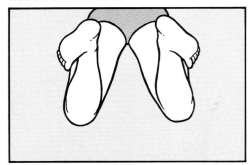

Cock the feet.

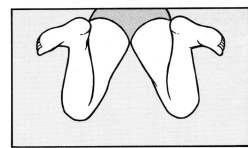

Outsweep begins.

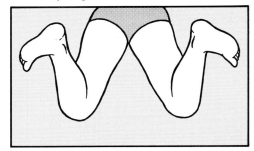

Strong Outsweep.

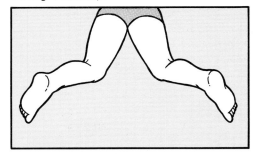

Downsweep.

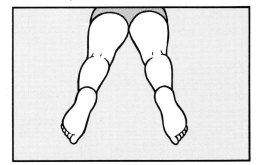

Insweep.

BREATHING

Swimmers who hold their head clear of the water should remember to breathe normally and regularly. Otherwise your breathing must take account of the natural body movements. The best time to breathe is when the shoulders rise during the strong Insweep phase of the arm action, and as the head moves clear of the water. In the early learning period, practise breathing out into the water when the arms reach Extension. This will allow you to breathe in fully whilst your face is clear of the water.

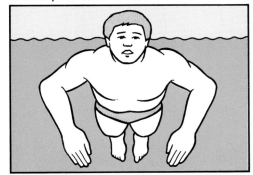

Shoulders rise at Insweep phase.

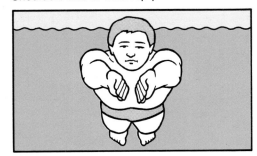

Breathe out when arms extend.

TIMING

As propulsion in breaststroke comes from both arms and legs, effective timing is very important. So work on your timing continuously. For competitive swimmers there should be no pause during the stroke, and at the end of the arm pull there should be a smooth transition to the strong leg kick.

Make sure that the leg kick is complete by the time the arms are extended, and that following the arm pull the leg kick is ready to take over. Once you can swim competently at speed, you may find that there is a slight overlap, with the arm action starting slightly before the leg action is complete. This is acceptable, and will develop naturally.

When learning, slow down the action of the arms and legs to ensure that co-ordination is achieved. Pause deliberately at Extension of the arms. The length of the pause can be reduced as the skill improves.

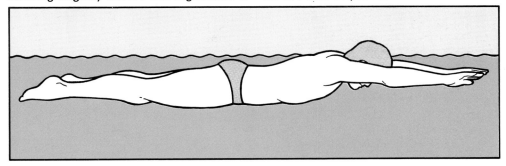

The leg kick is complete, the arms are extended.

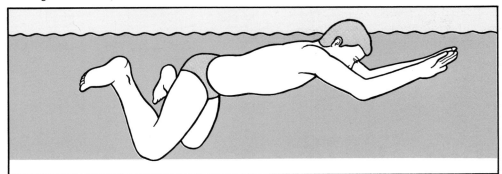

After the arm pull, the leg kick is ready to take over.

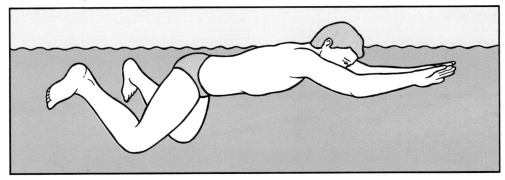

The legs kick as the arms recover.

SKILL AQUISITION

Breaststroke is probably the most difficult stroke to perform really well. This is due to its intricate style, and the importance of timing in mastering the stroke. In the early stages, rings can be used to support the body around the tummy. This will allow you to concentrate on making circular movements with your hands. It may even be helpful to go through these first with a teacher, either in the water or on land. It is important to understand fully the circular nature of the movement, which you can compare to mixing a large bowl of cake mix.

It is important that the feet also develop a similar small circular movement. You can do this if you concentrate on moving the heels in a circle. It is helpful to isolate the legs by using a float held at arms' length in order to practise the leg action. In extreme cases, it may even be necessary to lie on a bench out of the water and to have

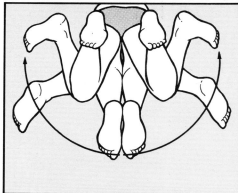

Make circular movements with your legs.

the legs manipulated by someone in the correct manner. In this way you can feel the movements required.

Once the circular movement of the legs becomes more natural, attention should then be given to achieving the flat foot position. Concepts like trapping a ball between the shin and the top of the foot whilst moving in a circle will be helpful here. But remember that as this is not a natural foot position, it is quite difficult for some swimmers to acquire this skill. So patience and perseverance are required.

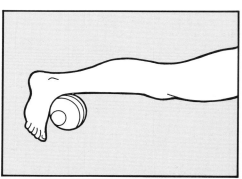

Foot cocked (dorsi-flexed).

Once both arm action and leg kicks are performed reasonably well, slow motion swimming will help to ensure that the timing is correct. Concentrate on completing the leg kick before the arm action starts. If you count the number of strokes over a set distance, this will ensure that the emphasis is placed early in the development stage on distance per stroke, which is so important in breaststroke swimming. Your aim will be to swim as fast as possible with a minimum number of strokes.

PRACTICES

Leg Kick

1. Use two floats, one held in each hand, to support the lower and upper arm. Lean forward and kick.
2. Arms extended, hold one float for-

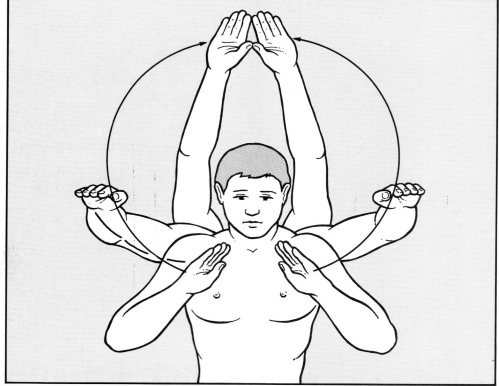

The circular arm action is a similar movement to mixing a cake.

ward, face clear of the water, practise the leg kick.

3. Arms extended in front, without float, practise the leg kick.
4. Arms extended at the hips, practise the leg kick, trying to touch heels with fingers to ensure heels are brought well up to seat.

Arm Action

1. With a rubber ring around the tummy, practise the stroke, concentrating on the arm action.
2. Repeat the practice described above, using a pull buoy, or similar aid, between the legs to enable the hips to remain high.

Timing

1. Swim the full stroke. Pause deliberately as the arms reach Extension to ensure the leg kick is complete.
2. Two kicks to one arm pull and permutations thereon.
3. Slow down the stroke movements to ensure that each phase of the stroke is complete.

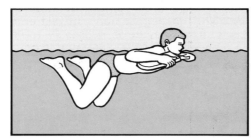
Leg Kick Practice no. 1.

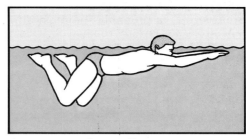
Leg Kick practice no. 3.

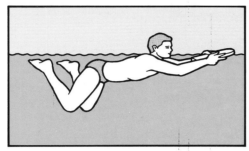
Leg Kick practice no. 2.

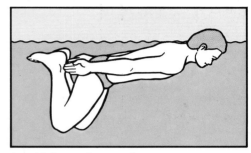
Leg Kick practice no. 4.

CHECK LIST

Body Position

1. Body as flat as possible.
2. Hips come to within 6″ (15 cm) of surface.
3. Arch back when breathing to keep hips high.
4. Feet finish propulsion about 18–24″ (45–60 cm) below surface.

Arm Action

1. Arms start at full stretch, hands touching.
2. Wrists flex and turn inwards at start.
3. During sideways movement arms press slightly downwards when hands pass outside width of elbows.
4. Wrists and forearms accelerate in movement.
5. Elbows remain high during inwards action.
6. When hands almost touching, elbow comes in.

Leg Kick

1. Legs recover together, toes extended.
2. Feet approach seat until directly above knees. Knees slightly apart.
3. Feet outwards, offering instep and lower legs to press on water.
4. Kick outward and backwards prior to strong inwards motion.
5. Legs reach full extension at end of kick.

Breathing

1. Inhale towards end of pulling action of arms.
2. Exhale as arms are pushed forwards near full stretch.

Timing

1. Arms, pull, legs recover.
2. Arms push forward, legs begin to kick back.
3. Arms at full stretch, legs finish backwards kick.

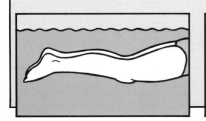
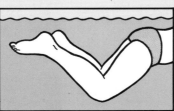
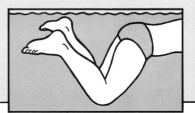
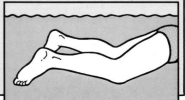

COMMON FAULTS

Body Position The hips are often held too low in the water. This is usually caused by the head being far too high. It can be corrected by establishing the correct head position. Similarly some swimmers let their bottoms bob out of the water when swimming. This can be caused by the head being a little too low, and by the legs being drawn up too vigorously towards the seat, with the knees forward of the hips. Correct this by altering the head position, and always make sure that the heels are brought up to the seat.

Some swimmers tend not to swim perfectly level on the breast. At the early stage, this is less important, but later on, especially for competitive swimming, it will be essential to develop this skill. Concentrate on swimming flat. This will be achieved by looking forward to a fixed point.

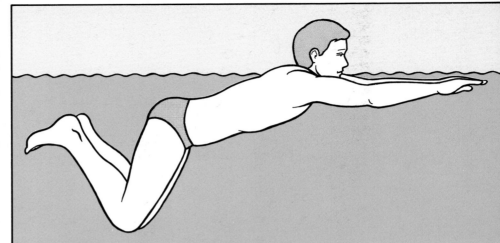

Avoid swimming with the head too high and the hips too low.

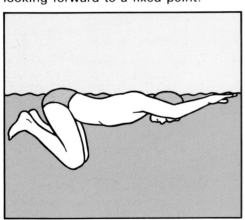

Head too low, bottom too high.

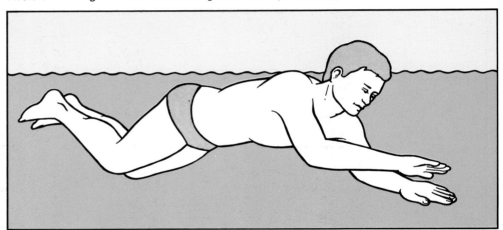

Twisted body position: not swimming on the breast.

Arm Action The major arm fault is usually pulling back too far beyond the shoulders. This can be corrected by concentrating on using small circular movements forward of the head.

Another fault is not reaching the extended position. It may be helpful in the early stages to pause slightly at the extended position to ensure that this position is achieved.

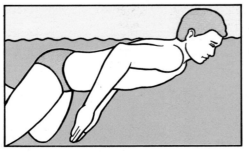

Pulling back too far.

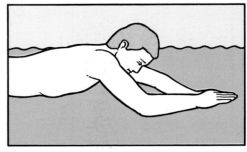

Not reaching extended position.

48

Breaststroke

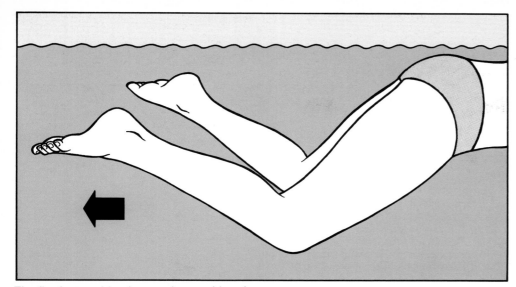

The flat foot position has not been achieved.

Breathing The main problem is breathing too early during the arm pull. Correct this by concentrating on breathing towards the end of the arm pull, and using the natural rise of the shoulders.

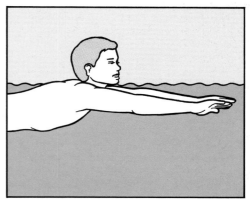

Breathing too early.

Leg Kick The main leg faults are that the legs do not work together, and that the flat foot position is not achieved. The only way to correct these is perseverance with the basic practise, and isolating the leg action by utilising floats and other aids until the skills have been acquired.

Timing The main problem is that the leg kick and the arm pull occur together, instead of the leg kick taking over from the arm pull at the end of its propulsive phase. Correct by introducing a pause into the arm pull at the extended position, to ensure that the leg kick is complete before the arm pull begins.

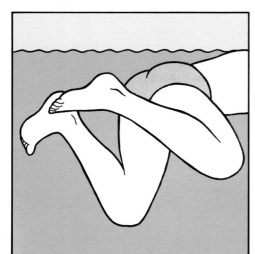

Legs not working together.

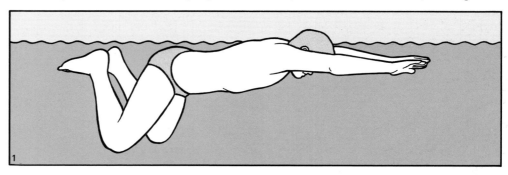

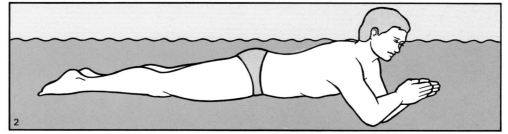

1. Arms at extension, the leg kick complete. 2. Arms and legs should recover together.

BUTTERFLY

Butterfly is the most demanding of the four swimming strokes. It is often the one which is learnt last when the swimmer has developed proficiency in the other strokes. In the early stages, swimmers often lack the physical strength to master butterfly. But once they have developed its natural rhythm, they often find that it is both enjoyable and easy to perform.

The casual observer of a good butterfly swimmer will note the flowing movements in the stroke, which appear to be effortless and without pause.

BODY POSITION

As the body position is continuously changing, it is impossible to refer to a stable body position. However, there are certain key features which must be present. The shoulders must be level with the water throughout the stroke to avoid disqualification in a race, and indeed to enable the stroke movements to be performed properly. The hips must be as close as possible to the surface, and the rise and fall of the hips should be minimized in order to reduce loss of streamlining.

As with all the other strokes, the key to a good body position is the movement of the head. The head should enter the water prior to entry of the arm for propulsion, to allow the hips to rise to the surface. When you lift the head to breathe towards the end of the propulsive phase, using the normal rise of the shoulder, this head lift must be kept to a minimum to prevent the hips from dropping excessively in the water. If these two points are observed and are backed up by a strong leg action, then undulation of the body will be reduced, and a smooth flowing movement will be attained.

ARM ACTION

Entry The hands enter the water in front of the shoulders. They should be pitched out at 45°, with a thumbs-first entry. If you flex the elbows slightly, you will enter the water smoothly and create as little splash as possible. Begin to move the hands outwards immediately after Entry.

Outsweep and Catch From the entry position in line with the shoulders, the hands begin to move outwards, extending until they are just outside the shoulder line. This initial action is not strongly propulsive, but ensures that

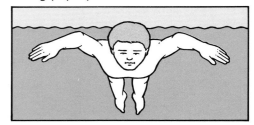

Good body position at Catch.

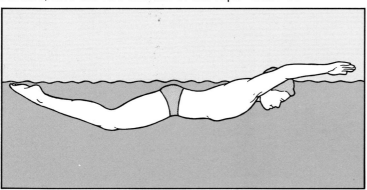

Hips high following Recovery.

Ideal body position (below).

Strong leg kick maintains high hip position.

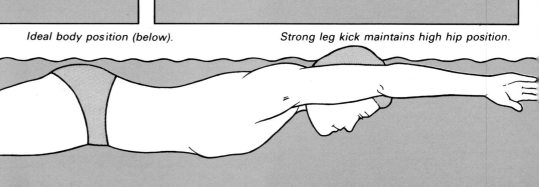

50

the hands are in a good position for the Catch, when the hands take a firm grip on the water. The Catch takes place with the arms extended.

Downsweep As soon as the hands have caught onto the water, begin to flex the elbows and change the pitch of the hands, while they move in a circular path down and out. This movement is completed as the hands reach their deepest point in the stroke. Then comes a smooth transition to the Insweep.

Insweep Change the hand pitch to inwards and backwards, as the hands sweep in together in an inward, upward and backward movement, with continued flexion of the elbows. The hands will come close together as they pass beneath the shoulders. Remember to keep the elbows high for maximum power from the strong back and shoulder muscles. As the hands pass the shoulders, gradually change the pitch.

Upsweep Then the Upsweep phase begins, and you should press back, out and up, backwards towards the thighs. The combination of these movements gives a stroke pattern similar to an hourglass effect, the shape of which will vary depending on the swimmer's strength and flexibility. Towards the end of the Upsweep, the elbows should leave the water before the arms are fully extended. As they approach the thighs, the hands should release the water by rotating inwards for a smooth Recovery.

Recovery Lift the hands from the water, and in a circular movement move both arms round low over the water, ready for Entry. You will make a better Recovery if the shoulders are clear of the water.

Whilst it is desirable that Recovery takes place low over the water, the hands must clear the surface to avoid disqualification. At this point, some swimmers will show a relaxed Recovery, with the elbows flexed, whilst others will need to extend their arms. Ideally, the movement should be as relaxed as possible, and should be performed with a minimum of effort.

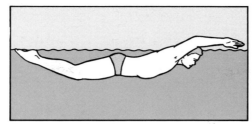

Arms prepare to enter.

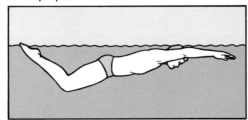

Outsweep.

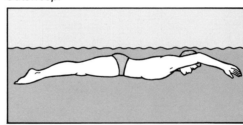

Catch.

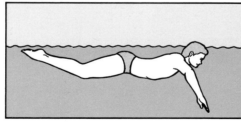

Downsweep.

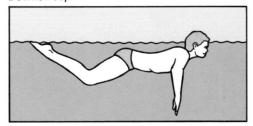

Insweep.

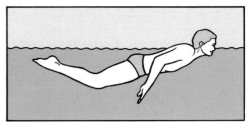

Upsweep.

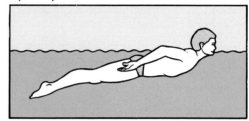

End of Upsweep. Hands release water.

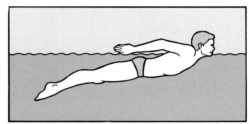

Recovery. Arms clearing water. Inhalation.

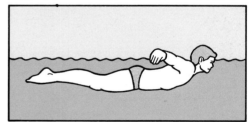

Arms recovering.

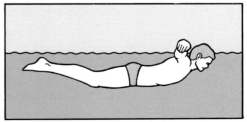

Arms passing shoulders.

LEG KICK

The main purpose of the leg kick is to keep the hips as high as possible on the surface of the water. It also contributes significantly to propulsion, particularly during the early phase of the arm action. The important points to remember are that both legs work simultaneously, and the main effort should come on the strong Downbeat.

Upbeat When it starts from its lowest point, the leg kick upwards is just a recovery movement, and offers little propulsion. At the beginning, there should be no flexion of the knees, and the feet should be in a normal position. When the legs are halfway to the surface, the lower legs should continue to rise, whilst the upper legs begin to move downwards. This means that the knees flex to prepare the legs for the strong Downbeat. Once the heels have broken the surface, you should flex the feet, and with a strong intoeing effect, start the Downbeat.

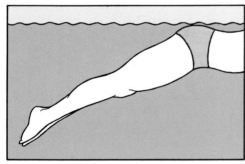

The Downbeat is complete.

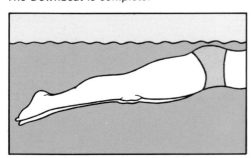

The legs begin to rise.

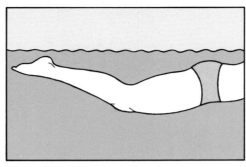

Upper leg down, lower leg starts up.

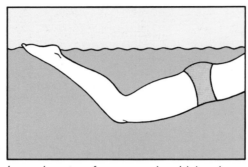

Lower leg at surface, upper leg driving down.

Downbeat The lower legs should now kick down from the surface in a strong whip-like action, catching up with the upper legs until they are extended at their maximum depth. Make sure that the legs keep together during the up and down movements, and do not part at all.

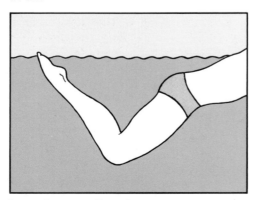

Lower leg starts Downbeat.

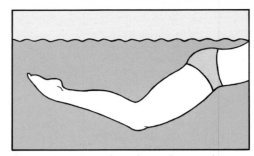

Strong Downbeat from lower leg continues.

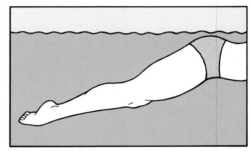

Strong Downbeat complete.

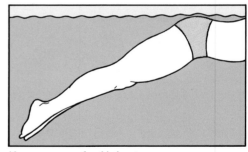

Kegs prepare for Upbeat.

BREATHING

As with the frontcrawl, breathing presents some difficulty, as lifting the head clear of the water destroys the ideal body position by forcing the hips lower in the water. The breathing movement should therefore be carefully controlled. It should begin at the start of the Upsweep in order to take advantage of the natural lift of the shoulders.

Extend the neck so that your head lifts gradually until the chin is just above the surface. This action must be complete by the end of the propulsive phase of the arm action. At this point you should inhale, and you should have taken in enough air by the time the arms begin to recover. This will ensure that the head enters the water again before the arms come round for Entry. When you drop the head, the hips will rise again for the important Entry/ Catch phase. Due to the nature of butterfly, breathing should be explosive (see page 29), as the swimmer needs a strong, firm chest from which to work.

The number of breaths you take is important for maintaining an effective body position. While the novice may need to breathe every stroke, the competent swimmer will develop a pattern of breathing alternate strokes. Remember that breathing must be forwards. Do not attempt to breathe to the side, as this can lead to problems with the shoulders dropping.

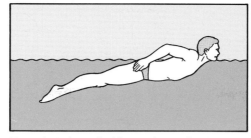

Extend neck until chin on the surface.

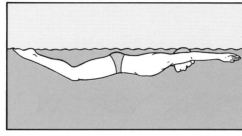

Head returns to water before hand Entry.

TIMING

Timing is critical if you are to develop a smooth, flowing stroke. It is difficult to teach, as it tends to come with practice. However, there are essential features to remember. There are two leg kicks to each arm cycle. The first leg kick is strongly propulsive, and is a vigorous Downbeat, which starts on Entry and finishes as the hands reach the Catch point. The second kick begins at the end of the Insweep, and is concluded as the hands complete the Upsweep. This kick is to keep the hips as close as possible to the surface.

There should be no pause during the arm cycle, which is often difficult for the novice. If you need to pause, due to lack of strength and endurance, you should do so at Entry. But the arm action should be accelerating, with a strong Upsweep phase, pressing back into Recovery.

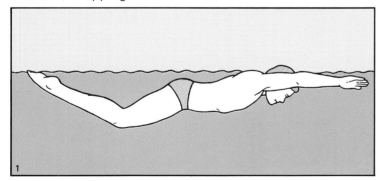

First Downbeat starts on hand Entry.

Second Downbeat starts as hand pass under the shoulders.

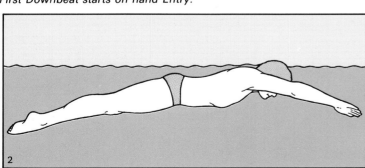

First Downbeat complete at Catch.

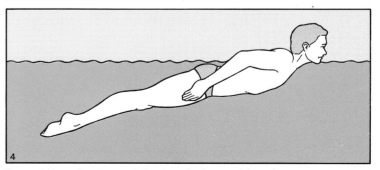

Second Downbeat complete at end of propulsive phase.

SKILL AQUISITION

Even if you decide to learn butterfly stroke last, some aspects of the stroke can be developed early on. For example, the leg action, which is relatively easy, can start to give you a feel and appreciation of the timing and of the movements themselves.

When learning the leg kick, you should make sure that it is initiated from the upper leg, and that a strong whip-like action occurs with the foot extended. Concentrate particularly on the strong downward kick. There are many ways of varying the leg practice to make it interesting—on the surface, underwater, swimming on the front or on the side.

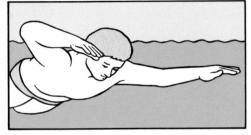

Progression: 1. single arm fly using right arm.

2. single arm butterfly using the left arm.

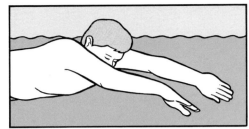

3. double arm pull follows.

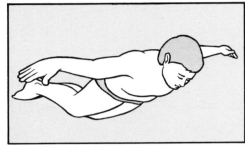

4. the arms recover.

There is no simple formula for learning butterfly. Endurance and strength are the essential ingredients for performing the stroke successfully. However, in the early stages there is a good way to perform a similar action to butterfly and to gain experience of the timing before attempting the double arm movement. Practise the single arm fly, with one arm extended forward, whilst the other arm performs the butterfly arm actions, and use the butterfly leg kick. During this practice, do not forget to breathe by lifting the head forward, and return the head to the water before arm Entry.

Once this skill has been mastered, then a combination of single and double arm practices can be employed. Use a single arm practice initially, with a short burst of double arm pulling, followed by further single arm practices whilst Recovery takes place. This will allow you to gain some momentum from the relatively easy single arm swimming, which in turn will assist and reduce the energy requirement for the short burst of double arm pulling.

As you improve, extend the length of time for double arm pulling. The breathing and timing skills should be integrated into this practice. Meanwhile do not forget the important points. Breathing takes place forward, with the chin

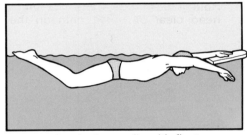

Practice the single arm fly with float.

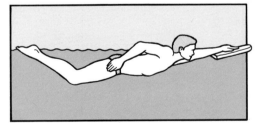

Breathe forward as propulsion complete.

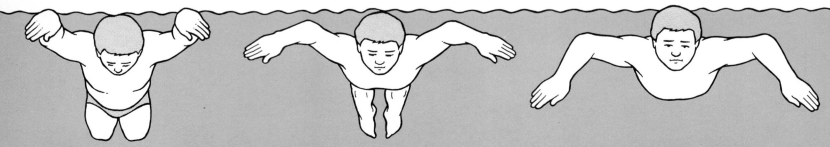

as close to the surface as possible and with the head being lifted as the propulsive phase of the arm action is complete. The head returns to the water before Entry. If you can match all this with strong leg kicks on Entry and towards the end of the propulsive phase, then the timing of will be mastered as the arm action is developed.

Throughout all the practices, concentrate on both arms doing the same action, and on a strong accelerating arm action, with Recovery clear of the surface of the water.

PRACTICES

Leg Kick

1. Hold a float with arms extended, head clear of water, chin on the water, practise the leg kick.
2. Arms extended forward, head in the water, practise the leg kick.
3. One arm extended, one arm at the side, practise the leg kick, kicking on the side.
4. Arms extended forward, swimming under water, practise the leg kick.

Arm Action

1. One arm extended or with arm at side, practise single arm butterfly swimming with a butterfly leg kick.
2. One arm extended forward, one arm butterfly swimming, use alternate arms.
3. Single arm butterfly, use alternate arms, integrated with occasional bursts of double arm pulling.
4. Swim full stroke without breathing for short periods.
5. Swim full stroke practising breathing action integrated with arm movement.

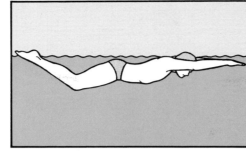

Leg practice no. 2.

Leg practice no. 3.

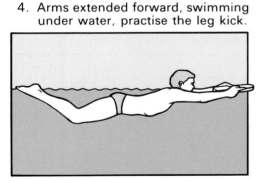

Leg practice no. 1.

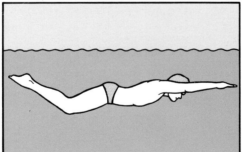

Leg practice no. 4.

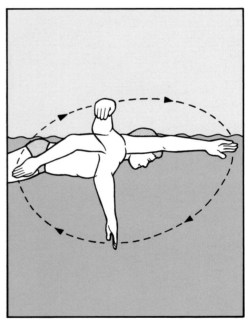

Continuous arm action.

COMMON FAULTS

Arm Action Many arm faults are due to lack of strength. Regular practice of the stroke will gradually remove these problems. Incorrect understanding of the precise action can also lead to difficulties, with Entry being made too wide, or by pulling with a straight arm. Both points should be corrected by verbal instruction from a teacher.

Leg Kick Many swimmers make the mistake of thinking that they will learn the stroke more easily if they use a breaststroke leg action. In fact, this often prevents development beyond the early stages, and should be discouraged by learning the butterfly leg action from the beginning.

The main leg fault is that the kick occurs by bending the knees instead of being initiated from the hips. A return to 'legs only' practice using a float may be necessary to ensure a strong kick starting from the hips. Concentrate on maintaining an extended foot position, particularly during the strong Downbeat action.

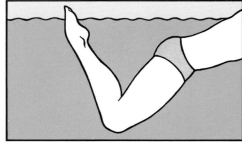

Excessive bending of the knees.

Breathing The major fault is to breathe at the wrong time. If you practise the full stroke, making sure that you breathe towards the end of the propulsive phase, you will be able to deal with this problem. Swimmers forget that the head must be returned to the water before arm Entry, and tend to lift their heads far too high to breathe. Concentrate on keeping the chin close to the surface to prevent this happening. The novice who finds it difficult to fit the breathing into the stroke pattern, will very often hold the head out of the water for too long. Correct this by using single arm practices to develop the basic timing skill.

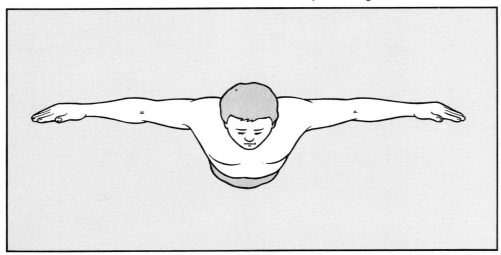

Avoid a wide Entry.

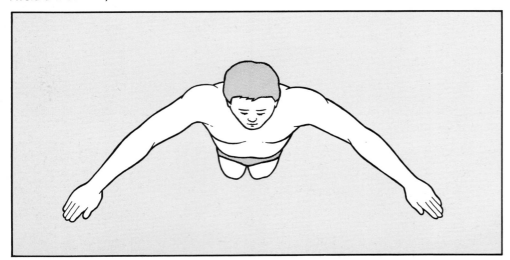

Avoid pulling with a straight arm.

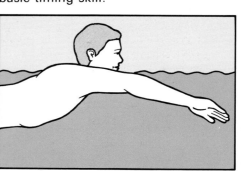

Breathing at the wrong time.

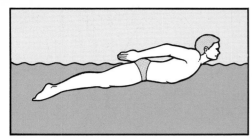

Head too high for breathing.

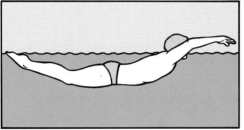

Head out of the water for too long.

Timing In addition to the points above on breathing, a common fault is failing to fit the two leg kicks into the stroke pattern. As the leg kicks both maintain a good body position and aid propulsion, they must be integrated properly. Single arm practices will help to develop the basic timing required.

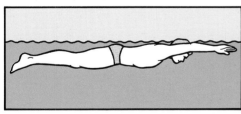

No keg kicks occuring at Entry/Catch.

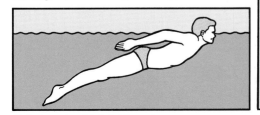

Only one leg kick taking place.

CHECK LIST

Body Position
1. Body horizontal
2. Top of head leading the way.
3. Slight undulation of whole body.
4. Hips close to surface.

Arm Action
1. Hands enter water before the shoulders.
2. Order of entry into water: thumbs, wrists, elbows.
3. Thumbs low on Entry and remain so for Catch.
4. Catch is outwards, sideways movement of the arm, with wrist firm and flexed.
5. Elbows remain high in water during the pull.
6. Hands should pull inwards under the shoulders.
7. Forearms pressed under body to the hips.
8. Arms straighten alongside hips for Recovery.
9. Elbows lead arms out of water.

Leg Kick
1. Strong whip-like action.
2. Legs remain together
3. Feet extended.
4. Feet turned in on Downbeat.
5. Legs slightly bent at top of kick at surface.
6. Legs straight at lowest point of kick.

Breathing
1. Inhale just before Recovery.
2. Exhale just after arm Entry.
3. Breathe once every two arm strokes.

Timing
1. Two kicks to every arm pull.
2. At Entry, knees bent, and feet at surface.
3. At Catch, legs straight, feet at lowest point.
4. As hands pass shoulder, knees bent, feet at surface.
5. Legs straight at end of arm action.

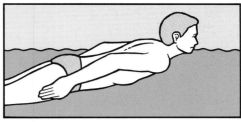

Breathing sequence: head begins to lift.

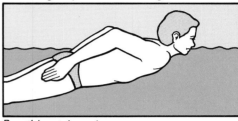

Breathing takes place.

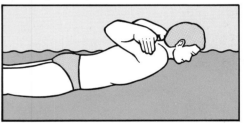

Head starts return to water.

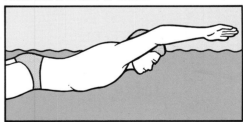

Face in water.

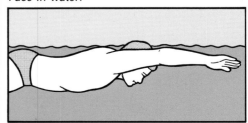

Hands enter the water.

STARTING TO DIVE

Diving is a completely separate skill which can lead you into a new challenge of both recreation an competition. Before you learn to dive, you should have mastered the basic swimming strokes, and be fully confident about submerging and swimming out of your depth.

Safety Before attempting any diving, you should consider the main safety points. Always make sure that there is adequate depth of water, particularly in the early stages. The depth will depend upon which dive you are doing. For the basic dive, there should be at least 2 feet (60 cm) more water than your stretched height with the arms extended. The flatter racing dives can be performed in shallower water. But never dive into water less than 39'' (1 metre) deep.

Always check that there are no other divers or swimmers in the area where you intend to dive. Awareness of others is important. After you have completed a dive, make sure that you can reach your point of safety without getting in the way of other divers. Never play around when diving, as this will lead to accidents.

THE FIRST STEPS

In order to perform good dives, you must be confident about submerging and swimming under water. Start off by revising the practices described on pages 17–19, and then go on to the practices described below, which are aimed specifically at developing confidence for diving.

Start by picking up objects from the bottom of the shallow end. Simply bend the knees and crouch on the bottom of the pool to pick up coins, weighted hoops or any other colourful and easily distinguished objects.

You must next learn to push and glide into the water. Stand with your back to the wall in water of shoulder depth. Lift one leg and place the foot against the wall. Extend your arms forward, place your head firmly between the arms and link your thumbs.

Lift the second leg to join the first one, and push off strongly from the wall. You will then move through the water. Provided you keep your legs together, and your head between your extended arms, you will glide for some distance without having to move arms or legs.

Repeat this several times concentrating on a strong push off, and thus trying to glide further through the water. You can then go on to gliding under the water. Start in the same way, but as you push off, drop your head about 2 feet (60 cm) under the water. Remember that the hands help in keeping the movement downwards. If you point the fingers towards the bottom of the pool, the rest of the body will follow.

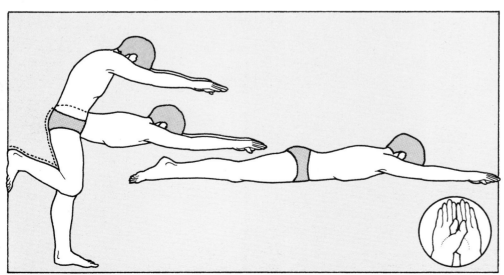

Learn first to push off and glide on the surface of the water.

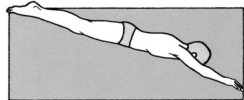
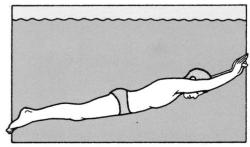

Then glide under water and surface.

As your glide slows down, lift the fingers towards the surface, and you will rise naturally. Do not lift the head. Only lift the head when you have broken the surface. Practice this technique of coming to the surface, as it will be useful later when diving in order to surface. Avoid the fault of not keeping the head between the arms.

In order to swim under water, when the glide slows down, simply carry out the arm action of breaststroke. This stroke should be longer than normal so that you pull through in a butterfly-type movement right to the thighs, and then recover close to the body to an extended position. The leg action under water can be as for breaststroke, but some people find a slow version of the frontcrawl leg kick easier. Your movements under water do not have to be symmetrial, but they must be propulsive.

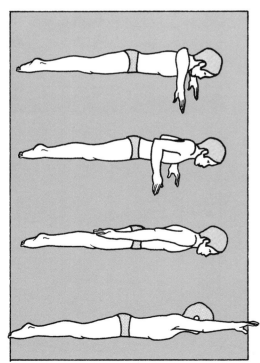

Swimming under water.

GAMES

To extend these skills you can have great fun inventing your own games. Try swimming through a series of hoops under water, or even create a slalom course, using floating poles. You can also swim between other people's legs.

However, always take care when swimming under water. Never do more than you are capable of, and do not hold your breath. Do not take several deep breaths before submerging. Just take one deep breath and then submerge. Keep movements slow and precise.

Handstands can be practised by pushing off the wall strongly into a glide towards the bottom of the pool. Place your hands on the bottom and allow your legs to rise vertically over the tops of your hands. Later, you can try walking on your hands.

If a friend holds out an arm at water level, you can spring over the arm. You need a strong drive from the bottom of the pool, and the body must bend between the hips and the trunk at an angle of around 130°. This is a basic body position in many dives, and it is useful to learn to control this angle.

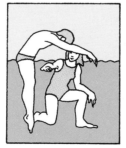

Learn to jump over a friend's arm.

THE SITTING DIVE

This is the first basic dive. Sit on the side of the pool with your weight as far forward as is comfortable. Place your feet on the bar and then extend your arms behind your head, with the thumbs locked together, and your head between the arms. Keep your head between your arms at all times. Point your arms towards the pool, and simply roll forward. As you leave the side, press firmly away with the feet. To surface, just lift your fingers towards the surface. This is a very shallow dive, and more like falling in.

The Sitting Dive.

THE KNEELING DIVE

Kneel on one knee, with the other foot raised so that it grips the edge of the pool. Bend the body forward as far as possible, but keep relaxed. Extend your arms behind the head and the thumbs locked as before. As the body over-balances, the foot on the pool edge pushes the body forward to enter the water. On entry remain fully extended to return to the surface. This is a deeper dive than the Sitting Dive.

The Kneeling Dive.

JUMPING PRACTICES

Before you proceed any further, it is a good idea to build extra confidence by developing basic jumping skills. Stand with the feet hip-width apart, and the toes firmly wrapped around the pool edge. Bend the knees and in one continuous movement push up firmly through the hips, attempting to gain maximum height. Keep the arms extended by your side, and enter the water as close to the poolside as possible, with the body perfectly vertical and looking forward.

To add fun and variety to this, try to gain maximum height and to jump as far out as possible. Never attempt to run and jump, as you could slip on the wet floor.

For the Star Jump, jump high into the air and push your arms and legs out like a star. Before you enter the water, try to put your arms down by your side and to close your legs. For the Tuck Jump, jump off the poolside with your arms by your side. As you reach maximum height, tuck up your knees as tight as possible into your chest and hold your knees with your hands. Before you enter the water, try to straigh-

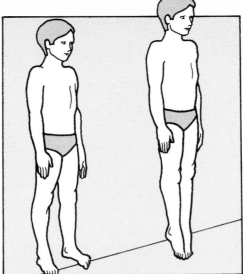

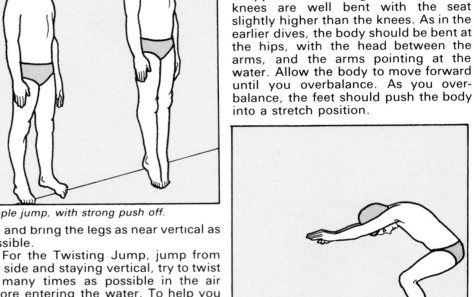

Simple jump, with strong push off.

ten and bring the legs as near vertical as possible.

For the Twisting Jump, jump from the side and staying vertical, try to twist as many times as possible in the air before entering the water. To help you twist faster, keep your hands close to your body, and swing one arm across the body, from right to left or left or left to right, as the case may be.

Star Jump, Tuck Jump and Twisting Jump.

THE SQUAT DIVE

This is the first dive where both feet are wrapped over the edge of the pool, the knees are well bent with the seat slightly higher than the knees. As in the earlier dives, the body should be bent at the hips, with the head between the arms, and the arms pointing at the water. Allow the body to move forward until you overbalance. As you overbalance, the feet should push the body into a stretch position.

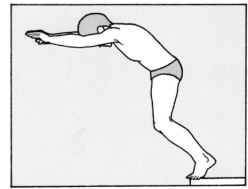

The Squat Dive with bent knees.

As you progress with this dive, you can raise the height of your seat and straighten the knees. Still keep the body bent forward. If you develop confidence quickly, you will find that you have reached a position where the knees are virtually straight and the feet have to be brought closer together. Remember that the knee flexion should be sufficient to allow a strong push off. The body must not overbalance at take off, when you should push the hips upwards.

As the height of the seat increases, the angle of entry into the water will increase until a vertical entry can be achieved. When your starting position is upright, you will need to introduce body flexion during flight, and then straighten the body just before entry.

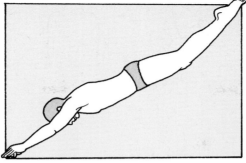

The Squat Dive with less knee flexion.

THE LUNGE DIVE

This is an alternative approach to diving progression, and it can be practised together with the Squat Dive. In some ways, the Lunge Dive follows on naturally from the Kneeling Dive and leads into a later dive called The Plunge.

The starting position is similar to the Kneel Dive, except that only the ball of the rear foot is in contact with the ground and the knee, although bent, is held slightly raised. Bend the body forward from the hips, hold the arms extended towards the water with the head between the arms.

As the body overbalances, propel it into the water at an angle of 45° using the legs and feet. Remember to push firmly with the leading foot to ensure that the hips go high, and also to keep the hands and head in the position already described.

As you become more confident, you can straighten the knees until they are only slightly bent and you are practically standing up. However, a slight bend is always necessary on the front leg to ensure a strong push off.

If you keep the body fully stretched during flight and streamlined in the water, you will progress a good distance across the pool. It is fun to check this distance. This flatter entry together with the glide will be an important feature of the racing dives, and leads us into the Plunge Dive described on page 64 of this book.

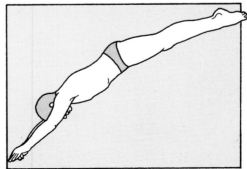

The Lunge Dive.

THE PLAIN HEADER

The Plain Header is the simplest of the competitive dives, and it is a natural progression from the skills described on the previous pages. As many of the techniques form the basis for later springboard diving, it is important that this dive is practised regularly until all the points are correct.

It is helpful to divide dives into distinct sections, and to consider each point separately, as follows:

Ready Position
Take Off
Flight
Entry

Ready Position Stand erect with your feet close together and the toes wrapped firmly round the pool edge. Raise the arms above the head and hold them in a wide position, with the hands at ten to two on the clock, the palms facing forward. The body should be perfectly erect, and the head in line with the body, with the eyes looking directly ahead and forward.

Take Off When you are ready to begin your dive, the first movement is to bend the knees slightly, thus transferring the body weight to the balls of the feet and keeping the hips directly over the ankles. The trunk will bend forward slightly. but the hands must remain in the wide position with the arms in line with the trunk. The degree of knee flexion will vary, but an angle of 130°–140° will give maximum thrust.

Once you reach flexion, it is important that a strong upwards drive takes place. There must be no pause in this movement, and the drive must be aimed to go through the hips. If correctly performed, the Take Off should ensure that the main thrust from the poolside is upwards.

Flight The slight hip bend should be maintained during flight. Only straighten the body just before you enter the water. Keep the legs close together, with the toes pointed, and hold the hands in a wide position in line with the upper trunk, with the head between the arms.

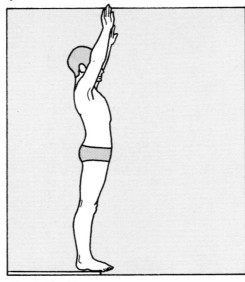

Ready Position.

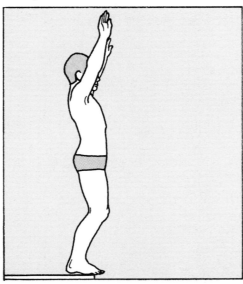

Take Off.

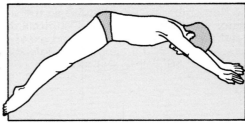

Maintain slight hip bend during Flight.

Straighten body just before Entry.

Entry.

Remember that the head is a crucial factor in diving and that a controlled head position is essential. Avoid excessive flexion of the hips. An angle of between 140°–150° will give an ideal flight. When you reach the highest point in the Flight and feel you are going downwards, try to spot the point of entry with your eyes, as this will enable you to begin correcting your body position for Entry.

Entry As the upper trunk moves down towards the water, you will sense the feeling that your feet are coming over the top of your body, and that your body weight is driving you down towards the water. At this stage, move your hands close together until your fingers are touching. If this is timed correctly, the fingers will meet just prior to entry. The body should straighten without any flexion so that your Entry is as near vertical as possible.

The head should remain between your arms in a normal position, with the top of your head entering the water after your finger tips, and with your toes passing through the hole made by your fingers. Try to avoid going beyond the vertical. If you vary the amount of flexion during Flight you will find that you can correct the angle of entry until the ideal vertical position is established. Maintain the entry position until your feet have completely submerged.

FAULTS AND CORRECTIONS

In order to spot your faults, it is most helpful if someone can watch you and give you some verbal correction. A good demonstration by a competent diver will also help to improve your technique.

Ready Position There are several faults associated with incorrect posture for the dive. Some of these are: the hands out of line with the trunk, the head forward, feet apart, back hollowed, legs bent and toes not wrapped round the edge. Practise taking up the Ready Position with your back firmly against a wall or even in front of a full-length mirror. Look at yourself both head-on and from the side.

Take Off It is the Take Off that dictates the rest of the dive. In the early stages, the main problem involves insufficient drive through the hips. If the problem is particularly bad, you should return to the simple jumping practises (see page 60), and concentrate on pushing through the hips. If there is insufficient drive, you will not achieve the right height for a good entry position.

Another problem which you may face is that as you lean forward during Take Off, your head will move out of line with the body, the arms will change position, and even flex too far forward. In fact it is difficult when performing the dive to appreciate where your body is. This is why an observer can help by referring to the drawings in this section. Remember not to bend the knees too much, and aim for an angle of 130°–140° for maximum drive. It could be helpful here to practise jumping up and down.

Flight You must learn to keep your body under control during Flight. Many faults are due to lack of body awareness. Opening the legs, bending the

knees and general body slackness are common problems in the early stages. Try to keep some tension in the body at all times. Even when jumping, it is important to have some tension in order to maintain a good body position.

Entry Many of the problems here are related to the problems in Take Off and Flight. Going over vertical at Entry is usually due to too much flexion during Flight. Again remember to maintain tension in the body throughout. It might be helpful to consciously stretch on Entry and to maintain this stretch until the feet have submerged. The hands not reaching together for Entry is a problem of timing. This can be easily solved by being more aware of where your hands should be. Other common faults are the legs crumpling on Entry or even coming apart. Once more, body awareness is the secret.

A bad Take Off.

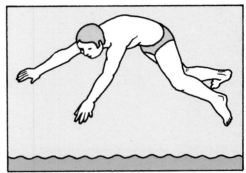

A bad Flight.

A bad Entry.

THE PLUNGE

The Plunge is not a competitive dive. But it is an essential dive to learn and practise, as it forms the basis for the racing starts described later, and provides for a relatively flat entry. It is simple to perform, and it can be quickly learned after you have acquired the skills of the Lunge Dive.

Ready Position Hold your feet hip-width apart with your toes wrapped round the edge, and your hips firmly over your feet. Your knees should be slightly flexed to 130°–140°, your trunk leaning forward, and your arms hanging down pointing towards the pool, with the palms facing backwards. Make sure that your body weight is as far forward as possible. Hold the head slightly down, with the chin quite close to the chest, and the eyes looking for a point of entry about 6½ feet (2 metres)

Ready Position.

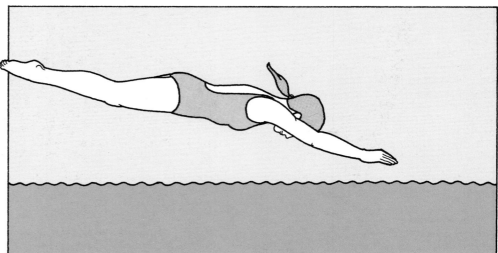

Flight.

Take Off.

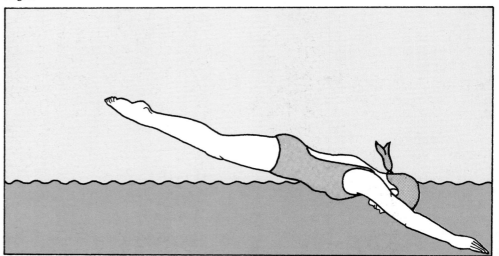

Entry.

from the poolside. When you are ready to dive, the emphasis should move towards speed.

Take Off To ensure a strong drive from the poolside the actions here should be vigorous. Swing the hands forward and drop the head slightly to between the arms, with the hands close together. This initial movement will bring your centre of gravity over the poolside, and will cause your body to roll forward. It may also slightly increase knee flexion, and as soon as you feel your knees approaching the level of your ankles, you should drive away from the poolside. It is important to use the arm swing to ensure a fast vigorous movement, followed by a very strong drive from the legs.

Flight As soon as you have left the side, try to streamline your body. However, as you go through Flight, it will be necessary to flex your body slightly to achieve a good entry position. Hold the hands close together in line with the head, and keep the legs streamlined, with the feet together and toes pointed. Flight should be low over the top of the water, aiming for an entry angle of 15°–20°. If you hold the legs streamlined here, you will ensure that the fingers enter the water first.

Entry The fingers should penetrate the water first. The head should be held between the arms, with the top of the head following the hands and arms into the water. There should be no flexion of the body at all at this stage and the body should be held streamlined so that the feet pass through the same hole made by the hands.

In practise, you will find it difficult to achieve Entry through the same hole made by the hands, due to the low angle of entry. But you should always aim for the ideal. As soon as you have entered the water and your feet are fully submerged, you can return to the surface by simply tilting your hands upwards and lifting your head. However, this should not be rushed, and a smooth transition from the glide is desirable.

FAULTS AND CORRECTIONS

It is helpful if someone can watch you as you dive, and point out the faults which need correcting. A good demonstration of the dive is also useful.

Ready Position The major fault is usually being somewhat unbalanced at the start. Remember to keep the toes firmly wrapped round the pool edge so that you do not slip. This also ensures that you always maintain good firm contact with the poolside. Taking up the correct position in front of the mirror is useful for improving your posture.

Take Off The Take Off will dictate the success of your dive. Many problems are due to lack of confidence, and can stem from the head being held too high. This will cause a flat Entry (belly flop), not pushing off hard enough, or even pushing off too soon making your Flight too high. To get a correct Flight, you should try to time your drive away to when your knees are level with your ankles. If you need extra confidence, it may be helpful to return to the Lunge Dive at this stage, where you can concentrate on the strong push off the poolside.

Flight Although it is necessary to have some slight flexion in order to successfully master the dive, the main problem with Flight is excessive flexion of the hips. This causes the feet to enter the water before the hands. When passing the peak of the curve, consciously try to lift your legs up high over the peak of the curve to ensure that they are in the correct position for Entry.

Entry This is where body awareness is particularly important. If you ensure that your hands are close together, this gives a good reference point, with your head firmly held between your arms. Try to pierce the water, and allow your whole body to go through the same hole. Make no attempt to hollow your back.

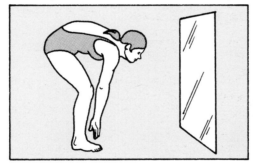

Practice the Ready Position.

A bad Flight.

A bad Take Off.

A bad Entry.

OTHER DIVES

Once you have reached a good standard in basic diving, you will no doubt want to develop new skills. There are many other forms of diving which you can learn, but unfortunately there is insufficient room here to cover these fully. The following are some of the more simple dives which you can practise without much help.

The techniques required for springboard diving are a little different to those for diving from the poolside. It is important to start by getting used to the action of the board. This can perhaps best be learned by practising a simple forward jump from the board using the spring. After this, you can practise jumping backwards, and then a Running Jump can be worked on. In this way you will understand how to use the board properly to improve your diving.

BOARD FORWARD JUMP

Before moving on to the springboard itself, you should start by practising carefully the movements described here

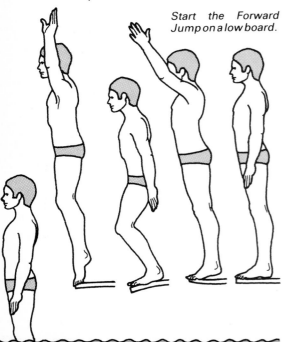

Start the Forward Jump on a low board.

on the land. After you feel that you have mastered them, and a friend has watched you and checked the movements against the drawings, you may then move to the springboard. Start on the low springboard which will be 39 inches (1 metre) from the water. Only when you have thoroughly mastered the movements, should you move on to the higher board at 10 feet (3 metres). Remember that patience is important in diving, as it is very easy to hurt yourself by progressing too quickly before skills have been well rehearsed.

The Ready Position Move up to the end of the springboard. Keep your body as vertical as possible, with your arms by your side. The head should be in line with the body with the eyes looking forward, and the feet firmly placed on the board, with the toes gripping the edge. If it is not uncomfortable for you, place your heels close together. However if the feet are slightly apart, this will not cause too many problems.

First Arm Swing The initial movement is for the arms to move upwards and sideways. As the hands pass your shoulders, raise the heels off the board until you are standing on your toes. This action should cause the board to move slightly upwards. However, remember to stay in contact with the board at this point.

The Knee Bend The knees should now begin to flex and the arms swing down and sideways, moving behind the hips. This will cause the board to move downwards. Maintain this crouch position until you feel that the board has reached its lowest point.

The Drive As soon as the board has reached its lowest point, move the arms vigorously forwards and upwards past the thighs to take up a position similar to that for a Plain Header with the hands held at ten to two (wide position). At the same time extend the knees vigorously. Your body weight should be firmly over your feet at this stage. If you manage the timing correctly, this strong final drive from the board will coincide with the upwards movement of the board and give you maximum height. As soon as your feet leave the board, point your toes and attempt to get into a vertical position ready for entry. Move your hands swiftly down towards your side, with your head in line with your body.

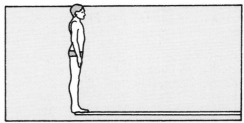

Ready position for a Backwards Jump.

The movements of the Backwards Jump are very similar, except that you start by taking up the position on the board backwards. Try to get the heels projecting a little way beyond the edge of the board during the ready position, while still keeping your body weight firmly over the balls of your feet. This can be achieved by leaning forward slightly.

You will find that it is a little more difficult to maintain a vertical entry during a backwards jump. However, if you keep your head in a natural position and make no attempt to look down, it will be much easier.

Ask to have someone to observe your technique points, paying careful attention to the drawings. Most of the faults with these dives are associated with the initial build-up: a jerky armswing, leaning excessively forwards or backwards during the movement, and not making full use of the natural deflexion of the board.

BOARD RUNNING JUMP

After you have mastered jumping from a standing position on the springboard, it is a good idea to move on to the more difficult Running Jump.

The Ready Position Stand in an upright position, a measured distance from the edge of the board. This distance will depend on the length of your run, and it will be necessary to pace this out before you start to dive. Practise this a few times before actually jumping into the water, to ensure that the distance is correct.

The Walk consists of three or four normal walking steps. The last step however, can be a little faster and a little longer than the others, as this is the one which prepares for the Hurdle Step. Keep your body upright, with your eyes focussed well ahead, and make no attempt to flex the body. Keep your arms close by your side in a relaxed manner. Some people find it helpful to move their arms in a normal walking fashion. If you wish to swing both arms together, this movement must be well controlled.

The Hurdle Step The final movement as you move towards the end of the board is in the form of a hurdle jump. As you take the last step, the trailing leg is brought forward and raised into a hurdle position with the knee in line with the hips, and the lower leg hanging down vertically. As this is done, swing the arms up vigorously into the Y position. At this stage, the whole body will begin to leave the board. Height is important here. The head should remain in its normal position, although the eyes should begin to focus on the end of the board.

Ideally you should aim to gain as much height as possible and eventually to land on the balls of the feet as close to the end of the board as possible. As you reach maximum height, the hurdle leg should begin to straighten to come together with the trailing legs so that both feet meet the board together.

Never attempt to stamp the board. The descent should be controlled. As you land, the board will begin to move downwards. The arms should also move down and out to behind the thighs, to ensure maximum deflexion of the board. As the board goes down, the arms should begin to swing vigorously forwards and upwards.

The Drive Your arms should now be moving forward vigorously and your knees are flexed with the board at its lowest point. It is important to concentrate on using the flexibility of the board to its maximum advantage. Reach forward with your arms into the Y position, and drive strongly off the board. For a good jumping entry, with your body as near vertical as possible, move the arms down towards your side so that you enter feet first with your head in line.

Once you have practised this, it will be possible to develop a running dive. As you reach the end of the board, simply dive in the manner described for the Plain Header on page 62. However, if you wish to progress further with springboard diving, it is best to find an experienced diving coach who will help you to develop the various special skills, and who will introduce to you the somersaults and twists which are used for competition work.

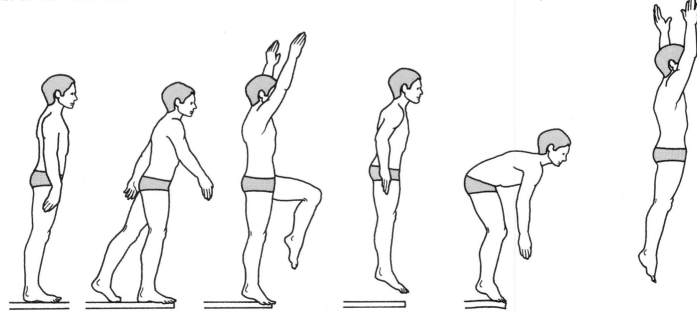

TUCKED FORWARD DIVE

The movements are similar to those described for the Plain Header, except that as you leave the pool side, the head is held in its normal position and the knees are flexed and pulled up towards the chest. As this takes place, move the hands down to grab the knees. This tucked position should be achieved as you reach maximum height. As soon as you reach this position, the hands leave the knees and move forward smoothly, and the legs straighten for entry. Remember that the eyes must spot the point of entry as they reach the highest point in the arc.

BACK DIVES

Backward diving is quite a big step, as this involves diving without being able to see the water. It may be helpful to do this in pairs, so that one person can check that you do not dive on top of someone swimming. Initially it is helpful to start from a basic crouch position.

For the Back Roll, take up a stance on the side of the pool, curled up with your toes firmly at the edge but with your heels lifted. Keep your head well down and steady yourself with your hands on the poolside. Then simply roll back into the water. With the head still down, grab your knees with your hands

as you roll backwards to make sure you stay in a crouched position. Remember to do this dive in deep water. Otherwise you may find you come a little too close to the bottom of the pool.

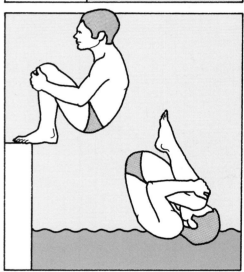

The Back Roll.

As soon as you feel confident doing this roll, you may wish to move to the next stage. Take up the crouch position on the poolside as described above, but as you fall backwards swing the arms out and stretch out by pushing your head back, arching your back and straightening your legs. This will get you into the position of a backward dive, and very soon you will find that from a crouched position, you will be able to move to virtually a standing

Tucked Forward Dive.

position for the drive off. By good arching of the back and throwing your arms up and towards the water, and also looking for the point of entry, you will achieve a reasonable backward dive.

FORWARD SOMERSAULTS

In order to develop a somersault from the poolside, go back to a simple Squat Dive. Take up a position on the pool side in a squat. Roll forward and you will find that quite naturally roll will be imparted. As you fall forward, simply remain in a tucked position, and somersaulting will be achieved. At first you will probably be a little nervous. Try to

remember to hold on to your legs and stay in a firm tucked position, and this will help you to achieve maximum somersault.

The next step is to stand on the edge, in a slightly crouched position. As soon as your feet leave the edge, tuck up into a ball and attempt to lean forward, again imparting roll. You will find that by placing your chin firmly on your chest, and driving your hips upwards and keeping your legs tight to your chest, the speed of the roll will be improved. A strong drive from the poolside is important to achieve a good somersault. Remember to grasp your knees tightly throughout the dive to prevent you from unwinding, which would slow down the somersaulting.

Once you are happy with these dives, you may be able to return to the springboard to develop both the backward dive and the somersault. However these are outside the scope of this book, and you should seek the help of a teacher before you go any further.

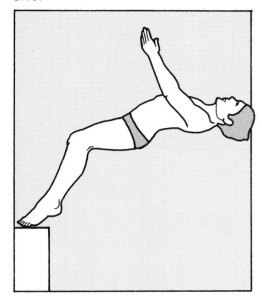

The Forward Roll.

The Back Dive.

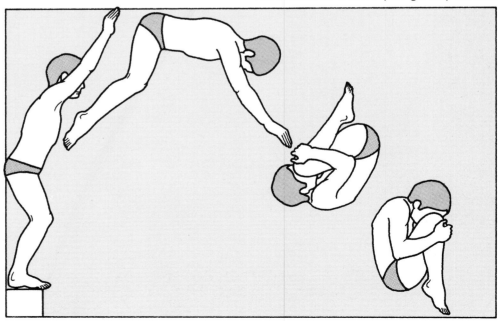

The Forward Somersault.

BASIC SAFETY

With more leisure time and changing lifestyles, the problem of drowning is a major one. Many people are losing their lives by not obeying the basic safety rules. Whether you are a swimmer or whether you take part in water sports, you must always appreciate the dangers of water.

Although there are many drowning accidents at the seaside, the figures show that the bulk of accidents today occur inland, in rivers, streams, ponds, lakes and reservoirs. Moreover, more accidents occur in the home than in public swimming pools.

GENERAL REMARKS

First of all, do not go swimming for at least 45–60 minutes after having a meal if you wish to avoid cramp developing. Secondly, always select equipment of good quality and safe design.

It is common sense not to play games involving the ducking of others. This can easily lead to water confidence being destroyed, and if your friends are nervous, it could put them off swimming for some time. Always have consideration for other swimmers, and avoid collisions wherever possible.

Do not duck others.

AT THE POOL

Many swimming pools have basic rules which should be observed, and often there is an attendant on duty to ensure that these rules are not broken. The rules are there for your own interest and for that of other swimmers, and should in no way inhibit your play in the water.

Running, jumping and chasing round the edge of the pool may be fun, but can lead to accidents, particularly if you slip from the poolside. Before jumping in, always check that the water is clear of other swimmers, and never risk a collision.

Do not chase along the poolside.

Be careful about using equipment in a crowded pool, particularly fins, flippers, snorkels and masks. Flippers moving fast through the water can cause considerable pain if someone runs into them. Snorkels have two possible dangers. If you are swimming under water, you can easily lose your sense of orientation and find yourself under the diving area. Also if someone swimming frontcrawl or butterfly for example knocks into you while you are using a snorkel, this will hurt them as well as injuring your own mouth. Always select one with a soft rubber mouth piece.

OPEN WATER

Always check that the area is safe for swimming. Ask someone working nearby, a beach superintendent, the local tourist office or even the police station.

On well-used beaches there are often warning notices, poles or flags indicating where you can swim. Many beaches are controlled by qualified lifeguards who place these markers to indicate where they can observe the swimming scene. Red flags are a sign that it is no longer safe to swim. Always obey these notices.

If you use a quiet beach, never bathe alone. Make sure there is someone watching you or swimming with you who can come to your aid in an emergency. Bathing at night is very romantic, but also dangerous. It is difficult to make out the shoreline and to see where it is safe to land. Remember there could be mud or even quicksand. Avoid swimming near piers and rocks, as strong currents build up around these obstructions, and can cause problems for the weak swimmer. Also as waves build up, you could be knocked against them and injured.

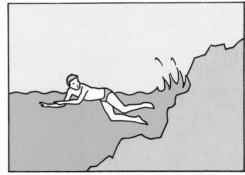

Do not swim near rocks.

When you swim in the sea you must know the local tidal conditions, and understand about currents and tides. Basic information can be easily obtained at most resorts. You should be aware of whether the tide is coming in or going out.

Do not swim away from a capsized boat.

Always try to swim parallel with the shoreline, and remember that it is dangerous to swim directly out to sea. Remember as you swim out that the same distance must be covered to return to safety. If the tide is going out, it will be more difficult to swim back to shore than to swim out. You could easily find that you have insufficient strength to get back. Even the strongest swimmer can find himself in difficulties against a tide, and it is only too easy to be caught.

Do not swim directly out to sea.

With young children, it is a good idea to tie an aid such as a rubber ring to a line, which can be held by a parent or relation. Rings and airbeds can easily be carried out with the tide.

Finally, do not forget the other dangers around you. Often there are surf boards, wind-surfers and boats on the same beaches as swimmers. Keep away from power boats. Boats cannot change direction very quickly and often cannot spot a swimmer in the water.

AT HOME

It is amazing to think that it is easy to drown in water at home. It is important to take precautions, particularly when young children are around. Remember that when you were young, you were just as attracted to water as they are. Do not leave children to their own devices. Garden ponds should be securely fenced or covered. Water butts must

always be covered. Never leave children unattended in a bath, or leave a bath full of water when children are around. Very young children have also drowned in washing machines and buckets.

Do not leave garden ponds uncovered.

WATER SPORTS

Many people enjoy taking out a boat from time to time on a river, lake or at the seaside. Since we are not all strong swimmers, it is important to observe commonsense safety procedures.

Before going in a boat, find out details of tides, currents and general conditions. At the seaside, you can get good information from the boat-hirer provided he is reliable, the local coast-guard or the harbour master. As mentioned above, you must understand about tides and what they are doing.

Always remember that weather conditions at sea are far different from those on land. Even if the weather appears good, take protective clothing with you. Weather can change quickly. Keep your eyes open for clouds building up, the wind freshening and the waves becoming bigger, possibly with foam. If conditions deteriorate this far, you should return to shore and safety.

You should wear a life jacket or buoyancy aid, which should conform to the relevant National Standards. Make sure that it is fitted correctly and that it is secure. Even the strongest swimmers

will find it difficult to stay afloat if they have to stay in the water for any length of time.

Never hire boats which in any way look inferior. Always insist on good quality equipment. Overloading a boat can lead to problems too. Most boats have a recommended number of passengers, and this should not be exceeded.

It is a good idea to give details of your trip to someone on the shore, perhaps the person you are hiring the boat from, your hotel or a friend. Tell them your anticipated return time, so that if you are delayed there is some information in order to start a search.

If you do capsize or fall in, do not panic. Always stay with the boat and make no attempt to swim to the shore. If you are wearing heavy clothing or shoes, these should be discarded. Keep your movements to a minimum. If you move too much, you will lose body heat. If possible, tuck up to reduce heat loss.

If you go canoeing, always take someone with you. Avoid rocks and weirs, particularly in the early stages. Wear the right equipment, a good lifejacket and a crash helmet to protect your head. It is advisable to have a proper training in the sport.

Fishing alone can also be dangerous. At the sea, avoid areas where the rocks are crumbling or where the foothold is not firm. You should also avoid coves which can be easily cut off by the tide. Again, remember to obtain accurate local information.

SKILLS FOR SAFETY

If you have followed carefully the instructions given in this book, you will now have achieved some efficiency in all the strokes and be able to perform simple diving routines. However, in order to be a complete swimmer, there are other skills which you will find helpful, not only for your swimming, but also for the sake of safety. If you take part in any activities in open water such as boating, windsurfing or water-skiing, you will need to develop the skills described below in this section.

ADAPTED JUMPING

In the **Diving** section (see page 60) we discussed how to effect a good jump into the water. But you should never jump into water where the depth is uncertain, or if you are not sure if there are any objects in the water. In the Rescue section (see page 78) we point out that it is better to wade into water rather than to jump. As this is not always practical, we must look at two possible ways of jumping in with safety.
Straddle Jump This is the shallowest jump available. It can be performed from a relatively low height up to about 4 feet (120 cm). Simply step out into the water and keep your legs apart, one leg forward and one leg back. Keep your head upright with your eyes looking forward, but with the trunk leaning

slightly forward at an angle of about 15°, and the arms held out sideways, level with the shoulders. This position will increase the area of your body which hits the water, and will prevent you from sinking too deep. As you enter the water, press down firmly with your hands and also try to close your legs slightly. This will create an upward force, which will further stop you from sinking.
Although this is a shallow jump, you should practise it first in a depth similar to that for diving—at least 2 feet (60 cm) deeper than your height with your arms stretched. Sudden contact with a pool floor can lead to serious injury.
Tuck Jump If you use the Straddle Jump from a height of more than 4 feet (120 cm), you will find it extremely

painful landing in the water. A more controlled entry can be achieved with the Tuck Jump.
Start as if you were going to perform a simple jump, as described on page 60, with your feet hip width apart and your arms by your side. After you have left your jumping position, immediately draw up the knees towards the chest and wrap your arms around the knees. Keep your head upright and remain in a tucked position, with the feet entering the water first. In this way you will make a slightly deeper entry, and you will avoid hurting yourself.

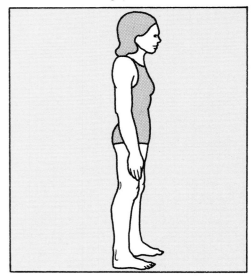

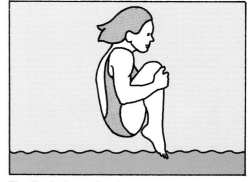

The Tuck Jump for deeper water.

The Straddle Jump is safest for jumping into shallow water.

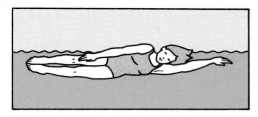

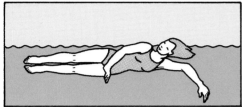

SAFETY SWIMMING

There are two useful strokes, both adaptations of breaststroke, which you should learn as soon as you can. They are very relaxing and valuable for swimming long distances.

Sidestroke avoids the fatigue of the other strokes, as the recovery of the arm action takes places under water. It is particularly useful for swimming with clothes on.

For the arm action, the leading (lower) arm pulls from the extended position in front of the head to level with the shoulders, while the upper arm bends to meet it. As the leading arm extends, push the upper arm back to the thighs. This is an alternate arm action.

The leg action is rather like a scissor action. Draw the leg nearest to the surface up towards your chest by bending the knee, while you push back with the lower leg flexing slightly. Then close the legs together.

For the timing, the legs part as the leading arm completes its pull, and drive together as this arm goes forward to extension.

Backstroke This stroke is sometimes known as Inverted Breaststroke or Life-Saving Backstroke. It is not only relaxing for long-distance swimming, but can also be used in life-saving rescue routines for towing floats.

Swim on your back performing the basic breaststroke-like leg action. It is important not to try to maintain a high body position. Lift the head forward to incline the legs so that the knees remain below the surface of the water. The foot position is the same as that described for breaststroke, and it is essential to drive back strongly, although the stroke has a much slower tempo. Use the hands to help you, either by making small circular movements outside the hips in a sculling motion, or you can use the backstroke arm action with both arms moving together.

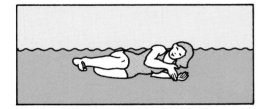

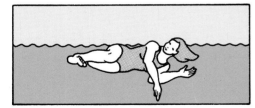

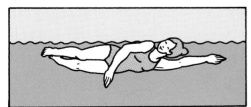

Sidestroke sequence.

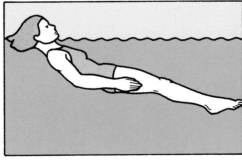

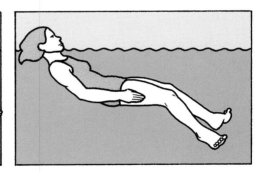

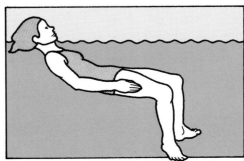

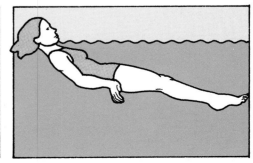

Backstroke is useful in life-saving.

TREADING WATER

When swimming in the pool or particularly in an open water situation when learning to sail, water ski or windsurf, it may be necessary for you to remain in the water in one place for some time. In order to be fully confident about this, you must develop the skill of treading water. There are various techniques, but the essential ingredient in all cases is to conserve energy and to be able to perform the skill with a minimum amount of effort.

Breaststroke Method Float vertically in the water and tilt your head back slightly to keep the mouth clear of the water. To maintain the head high, you need to perform a simple breaststroke leg action in a vertical manner. The movement does not have to be simultaneous or even symmetrical, and its only resemblance to breaststroke is the flat foot action.

Place the hands about 6–9'' (15–22 cm) beneath the water palms down, and press first inwards together and then outwards, just outside shoulder width in front of your chest. This action is similar to sculling. If you imagine you are stroking a dog, it will be easier. As you press out, the little finger should be higher than the thumb. As you press in, the thumb shoulder be higher than the little finger. All the time you should try to feel pressure on your hands. It should be done smoothly and continuously, but slowly.

Cycling Method The arm action is very similar to the breaststroke method. The head position is the same. But the legs need to imitate a cycling movement. Keep your feet at an angle of 90° to your shin, and imagine your foot is on a pedal. Again it is far better to keep the movement slow, and not to hurry.

Scissor Method This other simple method uses a similar arm action and head position to the breaststroke method. Here the legs perform a basic frontcrawl type kick. Keep the toes pointed, and make sure that the kick is continuous. Unlike the kick for the frontcrawl stroke, the kick does not have to be fast.

Skill Acquisition When starting to develop the skill, stay close to the side of the pool, preferably just out of your depth. At first you will find that you perform the movements too quickly, and that you soon become tired. Stop and rest.

As you learn to make the movements more precise, you can slow them down, and thus you will be able to carry on for longer periods of time. Always aim to extend the amount of time you are able to tread water, and try all the methods described above. Once you have found which method suits you best, this is the one that you should develop fully.

It is good to develop your capacities, as this can be a fun activity as well as helping the endurance factor. Once your leg kick has developed, try treading water without using your hands. To make life more difficult, one hand and forearm can be raised from the water, and then two. This means that you have to kick much harder to keep your head above the surface.

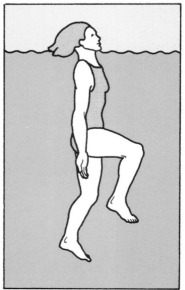

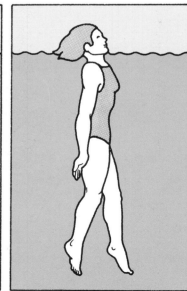

Treading Water: Breaststroke Method.

Treading Water: Cycling Method. *Treading Water: Scissor Method.*

SURFACE DIVING

In order to submerge when you are swimming or stationary, the simplest technique is to perform a surface dive. There are two main methods. Both should be practised for the sake of safety, and also because it is fun to be able to recover objects from the bottom of the pool.

Feet First Method This is the safest method to use when you do not know the depth of water. Start from the vertical float, and then perform a simple scissor kick, similar to a large front-crawl type kick, or a strong breaststroke kick. This will push your body high out of the water. Then hold your legs together, and as the body falls through the water your hands, which are held by the side, are pressed upwards in a strong outwards sweep.

The strong upwards sweep of the arms will propel your body under the water. To dive really deep, your arms should finish extended above your head. For shallower dives, the sweep can stop when your hands are level with the shoulders.

To start swimming under water, tuck up into a ball by drawing your knees up towards your chest, flexing at the hips until you are in a similar position to a mushroom float (see page 20). Then extend horizontally to swim.

Head First Method Start from the horizontal position, with the arms extended and the feet together. The first action is a strong breaststroke type pull through towards the thighs. As you do this, drive the head firmly down towards the bottom of the pool by pushing your chin into the chest.

This head movement together with the arm sweep will cause your legs to rise out of the water. As you feel your legs beginning to move above the surface, stop the breaststroke movement, change the direction of your hands and press firmly down towards the bottom of the pool. This will cause the legs to rotate higher until they are

vertical above your trunk. The weight of the legs will then push your body downwards. The hands must move forward together in line with the head.

When you have reached the desired depth, turn your fingers upwards. This

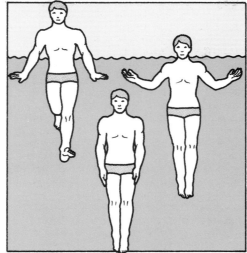

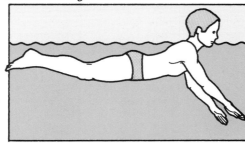

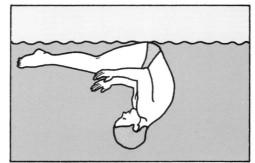

Surface Diving: Feet First Method.

Surface Diving: Head First Method.

will make you move horizontally instead of vertically. You can achieve a depth of 9 or 10 feet (3 metres) with this dive, but to go deeper you may need to perform extra arm and leg movements, as for underwater swimming.

UNDERWATER SWIMMING

Once you have learned to submerge, you need to develop the skill of underwater swimming. This is difficult because you have to learn to hold your breath (see page 59). It is important to conserve energy and that your movements are effective and slow. There is no particular action to be preferred, but the following variations are effective.

BREASTSTROKE METHOD

Use a long breaststroke action with the arms and legs. However, the arm action is an extended one, and the pull is similar to that described for butterfly. Pull through to the thighs and recover close to the body with the elbows held in. The timing is the same as for breaststroke, with a pull followed by an effective kick. Speed is not important.

BREASTSTROKE/CRAWL

This is a cross between frontcrawl and breaststroke. The arms perform a long breaststroke pull as described above. The legs perform an effective frontcrawl kick, but much slower than normal. This method is particularly useful if you find the breaststroke leg action difficult.

CRAWL METHOD

This is based on a dog paddle approach. The arms perform a simple dog paddle action, pushing forward from the shoulder and then pulling back like a paddle with alternate arms. The legs perform the frontcrawl action. This method is often preferred by sub-aqua

Streamlined entry with a smooth transition to swimming.

divers, and if developed correctly can be very effective.

STARTS AND TURNS

After you have dived in, it is essential to make a smooth transition from the glide to the swimming stroke. The point at which this transition occurs will depend upon which stroke you choose. It will take place early in the faster strokes such as frontcrawl, and it will be later for breaststroke. This principle also applies when you are coming out of your turns. As you progress, it will be helpful if someone can check your timing so that you achieve the best compromise.

For frontcrawl, the legs start kicking while the arms remain extended. Just before the head breaks the surface pull one arm downwards and backwards while the other arm remains forward. The body will come to the surface quite naturally, and then you can begin the smooth and continuous stroke. If you avoid turning the head in order to breathe, you will be able to establish a good stroke pattern from the start.

For butterfly, the legs start kicking before the arm stroke, as in frontcrawl. It is important to be able to judge the position of the body below the surface,

something which will only come with experience. This is because the arms have to be brought forward above the water. If you start the arm stroke too soon, you will find that recovery of the arms from the stretched position is impossible. Both arms should press on the water downwards and backwards into a continuous stroke movement.

For breaststroke, the rules allow a swimmer to take one stroke of the arms and legs while still under water, before surfacing. This is to be recommended, as it is much faster to swim under water than on the surface. You can practise this regularly every time you begin to swim breaststroke by pushing off under water and attempting the action described below. If you are a beginner, you can just surface and start swimming in the normal way.

As the speed of the glide reduces, pull backwards with a long arm stroke to the thighs, like in butterfly. This strong pull will accelerate the body and allow a second glide to take place, with the hands held by the thighs. The body will now be stretched, with the head in line and the arms beside the body.

As the second glide slows down, push the hands and arms forward close to the body to stretch out, and draw the heels up to the bottom to push back strongly. The legs should be completing the backwards kick as the arms reach the extended position and the head breaks the surface of the water. After this, a normal stroke pattern should be established. Never pause between the end of this first kick and starting to swim.

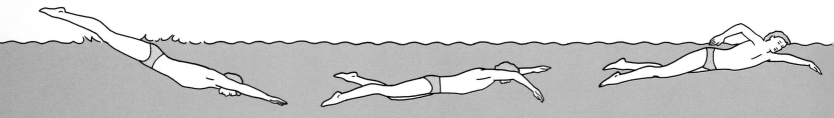

76

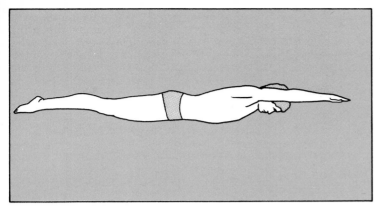

Breaststroke: first glide, arms extended.

Second glide, arms extended.

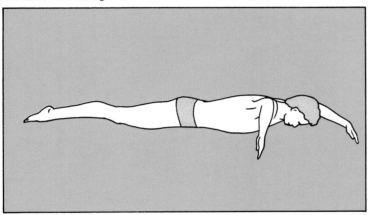

Strong pull with hands.

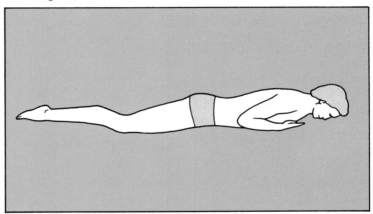

Arms recover close to body. Legs start to recover.

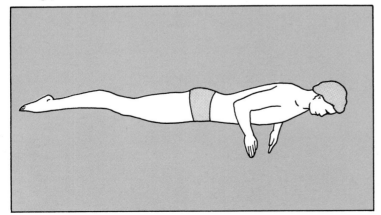

Hands continue to press backwards from shoulders.

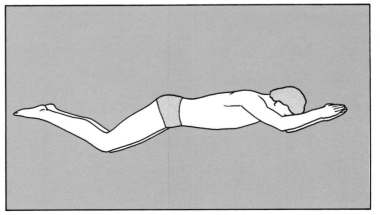

Hands move to extension. Legs still recover.

RESCUES

Once you have become a proficient swimmer, it will be useful to learn about the basic skills of helping others. One day you could find yourself in a position where someone needs your help, because they are not as competent a swimmer as you, or have over-extended themselves.

One important point to remember when you go to someone's aid is that you should not place yourself in danger. This only increases the difficulties, and could mean that you put your own life at risk. It is quite common for people who try to rescue others to get into difficulties themselves, while the person they have gone to rescue reaches safety. The following points are for your general guidance.

A golden rule is never to enter the water unless absolutely necessary. Nor should you come into contact with the person in difficulty unless absolutely necessary. Let us look at a few simple situations which can be dealt with easily.

CASUALTY NEARBY

It is surprising how often people find themselves in difficulty very close to land, not more than 10 feet (3 metres) out. If you simply extend your reach with a pole or a stick, this will enable the person to reach safety. It is important that his technique of extending your reach is done carefully.

Start by making sure that the casualty is aware of your presence. Attract his attention, and make it clear that you are there to help him. Make sure that he looks at you and keeps his head well clear of the water. If he is waving his hands, tell him to put them under the water. Remember that we float more easily with our hands under water.

You should select quickly what you are going to use to extend your reach. Ideally this should be something rigid like a pole or a branch. If this is not possible, you may need to use an item of clothing. Lie down on the side with your legs slightly apart, and if possible

at a slight angle to the shoreline. This will ensure that your centre of gravity is kept low, and will make it virtually impossible for the casualty to pull you into the water. Do not reach over the edge. If anybody is with you, get them to hold your feet carefully and to place their weight over your legs. Otherwise, if there is anything nearby that you can grab, hold on to it firmly to avoid being pulled in.

Give clear instructions to the person in the water. Tell him what to do: to grasp the pole firmly, to keep his hands under water, to kick with his legs and to keep his head clear of the water. As soon as he has taken hold of the pole or clothing, pull him in gently towards the side. If possible, let him take hold of the edge himself. If you have to give him help, wait until he is close to the shore and then grasp the back of his wrists. Once again, there must be no danger of you falling in.

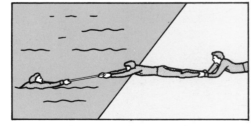
Using a pole to extend your reach.

Helping a casualty out of the water.

CASUALTY FURTHER OUT

Often reasonable swimmers get into difficulty simply through being tired or over-extended. In these cases you should throw them something that floats, for example a ball, a lifebelt or an empty squash bottle. With something to support them, they should be able to reach the shore by kicking their legs. This avoids you having to get into the water, and thus endangering yourself.

When effecting this rescue, the golden rules are simple. First communicate with the casualty. The things to tell them are: keep your hands in the water, keep your head up, keep calm, I am coming to help you. Explain clearly what you are going to do so that he knows what to expect, for example I am going to throw a ball.

Stand a little way back from the edge and throw the ball carefully. Keep your eye on the ball, and look where you want it to land. An underarm throw will usually be satisfactory. For longer distances you may have to use an overarm throw, although this makes the aim more difficult.

Once the casualty has got hold of the ball or float, tell him what to do: lean forward, kick your legs, come towards me. Try to avoid contact until he is very close to the side.

Ropes are useful for rescues, particularly where boats are concerned. Again communication is essential: keep your hands under the water, keep your head up. Always explain what you are going to do and what the casualty should do.

Coil the rope neatly into small coils. Avoid tangling it so that the first throw is correct. Hold on firmly to the loose end of the rope. It is helpful to place this under one foot, as it is easy to forget and throw the whole rope by mistake. With big heavy ropes throw in half of the coil, and hold the other half loosely in one hand. Throwing under arm is most accurate, and can be practised in your garden at home, placing an object on the lawn. Aim to be accurate from a distance of about 10 yards (8–10 metres) from the object.

As soon as the casualty has grabbed the rope, tell him clearly what to do: hold the rope with both hands, lean forward, kick your legs. Then pull him in gradually and smoothly. If you rush, you could in fact snatch the rope from his hands, or even slightly submerge him. A steady, continuous pull is best.

The best way to handle a rope.

Pulling in on a rope.

WADING RESCUE

If it is necessary to enter the water to effect a rescue, then you must remove shoes or heavy clothing so that you are as mobile as possible. If you are not sure of the conditions, lower yourself in gently and gradually feel your way along the bottom. Use a pole or stick to test the depth. A pole or stick or clothing are also useful in case you are

unable to get close to the casualty. Do not wade in beyond chest depth.

Again explain clearly what you are going to do. Make sure your feet are in a good strong stable position by standing with your legs apart, to avoid him pulling you over as he grabs the pole. If there are a number of people present, a human chain can be formed to give stability.

The best stance for a Wading Rescue.

SWIMMING RESCUE

If you have to swim to rescue a casualty, the golden rule is to avoid contact with him. So take buoyancy aids or clothing with you to pass to the casualty. If you offer a buoyancy aid, encourage him to use this to kick towards the shore. If you offer clothing, he can hang on to this while you swim a form of sidestroke along side, pulling him along as in a tow. Remember that you should always keep a good distance from him to avoid contact. Keep on giving encouragement, and tell him to kick to help him on his way.

If you wish to learn more about becoming a lifeguard or life saver, you should join your national association. The techniques of towing and making contact tows require considerable skill. Until you are proficient and understand the problems, you should not attempt contact rescues, as it could put your own life in danger.

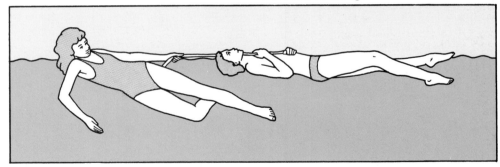

A swimming rescue using a piece of clothing.

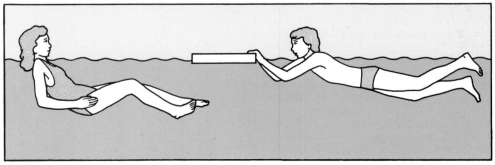

An accompanied rescue using a buoyancy aid.

RESUSCITATION

You may find yourself one day in a position where a casualty has been rescued, but is unconscious and not breathing, and needs your help. This can happen not only in the water, but also at work or even in the home. The technique of resuscitation is therefore something that we should all learn.

The golden rules of resuscitation are to keep calm, to start resuscitation as soon as practical, and to send for help if possible. The most effective as well as the simplest method of resuscitation is known as the Expired Air Method. It is easy to learn, and only requires one person to carry it out competently. No particular aids are required, and it has been found that it provides the best method of getting air into the lungs of the casualty.

Make sure first that the person really has stopped breathing. It is very painful for someone if you try to resuscitate them when they are still breathing. Apart from the obvious signs of lack of breathing, a certain blue discoloration on the face and lips is a good sign that there is a shortage of oxygen.

THE METHOD

The important thing is to get the casualty onto his back as quickly as possible. Then lift the jaw and tilt the head back as far as you can. This action may be sufficient to allow breathing to start again, as by doing this the tongue is brought clear of the wind pipe. If the

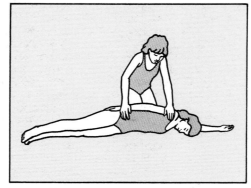
The casualty turned on the side.

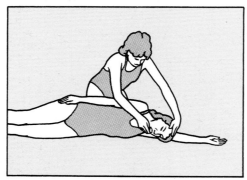
Clear the mouth of obstructions.

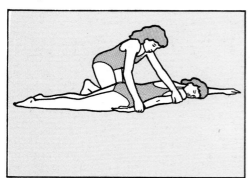
Starting to turn the casualty.

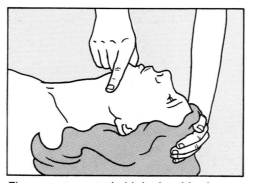
The correct way to hold the head back.

casualty is still not breathing, move on quickly to the next stage.

Check the mouth for any obstructions. Remove dentures if present, remembering to maintain the high head position. You can do this by placing one hand firmly on the casualty's forehead, while the other hand is placed around the chin with the index finger and thumb along the jaw bone, and the middle finger curled underneath the chin. You should also keep the little and second finger curled up to avoid putting pressure inadvertently on the throat. This could prevent resuscitation taking place.

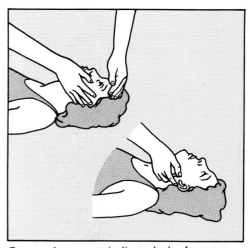
Eyes and ears can indicate lack of oxygen.

Then, keeping the casualty's mouth sealed, place your mouth over his nose, making sure that you effect a good seal. Start by giving four or five quick breaths in rapid succession in order to make sure that the maximum amount of oxygen is pushed into the lungs. Then raise your head and watch the chest for breathing out. After that, continue inflating the casualty at approximately five second intervals, and keep raising your head to observe the natural rise and fall of the chest. Carry on with this technique for as long as possible, or until breathing starts again.

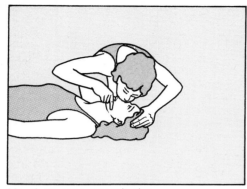
Mouth to nose resuscitation.

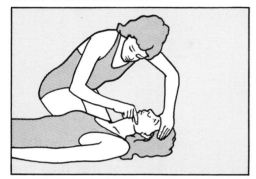
Look up regularly to observe the chest.

If mouth to nose resuscitation is not possible, then you will need to try mouth to mouth resuscitation. Press your hand on the casualty's forehead and effect a seal on the nose, and by

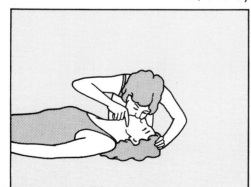
Mouth to mouth resuscitation.

pinching it firmly with the fingers of the same hand, blow firmly into his mouth in the manner described above. In other respects, the sequence is the same.

If the casualty vomits during resuscitation, which can often happen, simply roll him away from you until vomiting is complete. Then quickly clear the mouth of any debris left and return to resuscitation as quickly as possible.

RECOVERY POSITION

Once normal breathing has been established, place the casualty in the recovery position shown in the drawing. You will see that the lower leg is extended, and the upper knee is bent forward to act as support. The lower arm is extended behind the back, while the upper arm is flexed in front.

It is important at this stage to avoid pressure on the rib cage, and this

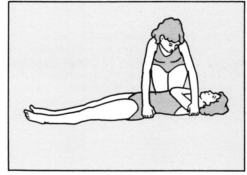
Start to turn the casualty.

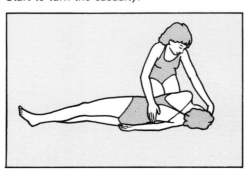
The casualty turned on the side.

position allows the person to recover slowly. Keep the casualty warm and under close observation all the time.

SKILL ACQUISITION

Since this is such an important skill, it is one that you should practice regularly with someone. You should feel confident about placing a casualty in the correct position for resuscitation and recovery. You should also be able to breathe deeply at regular intervals, and know how to place the head in the high tilted position.

When practising, remember never to blow into the nose or mouth. For mouth to nose resuscitation, blow on your partner's forehead, and for mouth to mouth blow along the far cheek. If you wish to simulate more realistically, dummies are available at most pools, or from voluntary organisations.

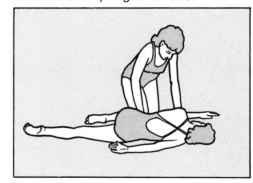
Place the casualty in the Recovery Position.

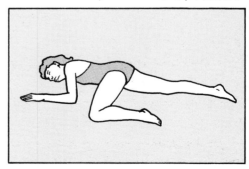
The correct Recovery Position.

WATER EXERCISES

If you are interested in general fitness, swimming is the perfect introduction to healthy exercise. Since the water offers support and buoyancy, this means that a complete beginner can embark on a programme of physical activity which will not cause too much stress.

Provided that you begin gently and do not attempt anything strenuous, it should not be necessary to visit your doctor before embarking on a simple fitness programme. Obviously if you have a history of heart trouble, blood pressure, chest problems, diabetes or any other serious disability, you should check on the advisability of starting a water fitness programme.

Whatever your level of swimming, it is a good idea to improve your level of fitness and also to organize your time at the pool to the best advantage. In this section we describe a series of exercises which are designed to give local muscular fitness. Start by selecting a few from each section. Once you can swim with confidence, you may want to combine the exercises with the swimming fitness programme described on page 86.

You should work out a programme which suits your own strength and ability. It is best to plan a variety of activities, which should include some relaxation as well as maintenance and improvement of ability. In this way, you will experience an overall increase of strength throughout the body.

If possible, practise the exercises twice a week. To begin with, limit the time spent in the water to around 20 minutes. You can gradually build up to nearly an hour, and perhaps visit the pool more often.

LEGS

1. Stand in the water and hold the bar with one hand. Lift first one foot and move it out, and then return it to the normal standing position. Do the same with the other foot. Repeat several times.
2. Lie on your stomach, hold the bar with both hands and allow your legs to rise to the surface in a floating position. When your legs are at the surface with the feet together, part them sideways and then press them together again. This exercise can be repeated on your back, again holding the bar.
3. Lie on your side, and hold the bar with one hand, while the other hand presses the wall about 12'' (30 cm) below the bar. Push down towards the pool bottom with your lower leg, and then lift it back to the surface.
4. Lie on your stomach holding the bar with both hands. Allow your legs to rise to the surface. Press first one leg down and then up to the surface. Then do the same with the other leg.
5. Stand in shoulder-depth water holding the bar with both hands. Raise each leg backwards and upwards.
6. Lie on your back holding the bar with both hands. Allow the legs to rise to the surface, and then press down with one leg towards the bottom of the pool. Do the same with the other leg.
7. Lie on your back holding the bar with both hands. Pull your trunk into a vertical position until the back is firmly against the wall. Keep your legs extended horizontally in the water. Then slowly raise and lower both legs together.
8. Lie on your back holding the bar with both hands. Keeping the feet at the surface, swing your legs together from side to side, just outside hip width.
9. Lie on your back holding the bar with both hands. Extend your feet at the surface, and then rotate your hips to put one leg over the top of the other. You should do this in both directions.

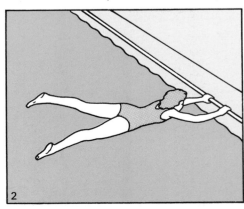

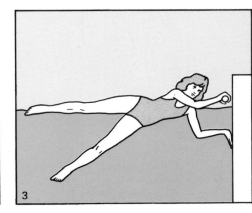

ARMS AND SHOULDERS

1. Stand in shoulder-depth water, with the feet firmly on the bottom. Extend your arms sideways on the surface of the water, level with the shoulders. Press both arms down towards the hips, and then raise them again until they are level with the shoulders.
2. Lie on your back with your toes hooked firmly under the bar. Float horizontally on the surface of the water, and put your arms by your side. Swing first one arm round in a semi-circular movement above your head, and then the other.
3. Lie on your back with your toes hooked firmly under the bar. Perform a simple backcrawl arm movement, but press down deeper into the pool than you would if performing the stroke.
4. Lie on your back with your toes hooked firmly under the bar. Keeping one arm by your side, try to push the other arm as far as possible up your back.
5. Lie on your stomach with your arms and legs extended, holding the bar with an over-grasp. Bend your arms so that you pull your body in towards the bar. When your head reaches the wall, straighten and extend the elbows.
6. Repeat the above exercise with an under-grasp on the bar.

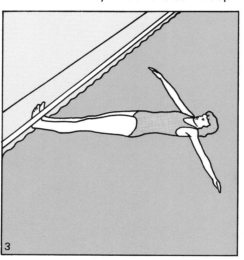

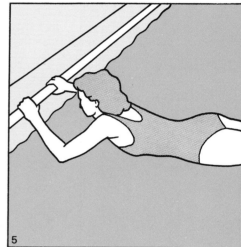

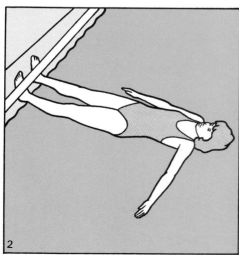

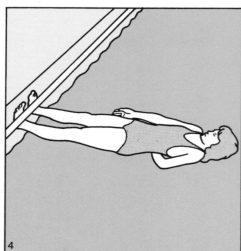

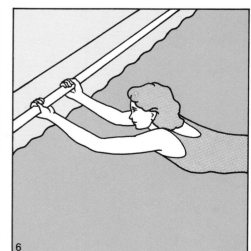

HIPS

1. Stand in the water and hold the bar securely. Bend one knee, lifting up the heel towards your bottom, and then straighten.
2. Lie on your stomach and hold the bar with both hands. Bend one knee, lifting the heel towards your bottom, and then straighten the leg.
3. Lie on your back holding the bar with arms extended. Bend one knee and drop the leg low into the water, and then straighten. Repeat using the other leg.
4. Stand in the water and hold the bar. Lift your knee forwards towards your chest and then straighten. Repeat with the other knee.
5. Lie on your side holding the bar with one hand, while the other hand presses the wall about 12'' (30 cm) below the bar. Bring the knee of the upper leg up towards the chest. Turn on the other side and repeat.

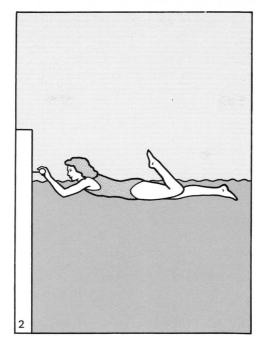

AEROBICS

Swimming is particularly helpful for the general improvement of heart and lungs. In order to achieve a satisfactory level of fitness, you should develop your own progressive programme, using extended swimming sessions. It is a good idea as well as socially rewarding to form a small group so that you can attend the pool together regularly.

TYPICAL SESSIONS

The amount and intensity of exercise needs to be developed slowly. Start off swimming short distances, and then gradually extend it. After that, you may want to work out a programme for yourself, using the examples below as guidance. These are based on a pool 27 yards (25 metres) long.

At no time should you feel over-stressed, particularly after the exercise period is complete. If you do get over-tired, this means that you should select an easier programme. You should therefore make a plan which fits in with your skill and experience. Never try to be too ambitious.

Easy This should take you roughly 20 minutes. Five minutes warm up. Five lengths frontcrawl leg kick using a float, with 45 seconds rest at the end of each length. Five lengths backcrawl, with 45 seconds rest between each length.

Swim continuously for three minutes, using any stroke/s, then rest for one minute. Two lengths easy swimming.

Medium This should take you roughly 30 minutes. Five minutes warm-up. Five lengths backcrawl, arms only using a pull buoy, with 30 seconds rest between each length. Five lengths backcrawl, legs only, resting for 30 seconds between each length. Concentrate on technique in both cases. Swim frontcrawl for 10 lengths without stopping, alternate fast and slow lengths. Five lengths fast breaststroke, resting for 45 seconds between each length. Four lengths easy swimming.

Hard This should take you 45–60 minutes. Five minutes warm-up. 10 lengths breaststroke, concentrating on technique, with 30 seconds rest between each length. 12 lengths frontcrawl, resting for 20 seconds every other length. 24 lengths backcrawl resting for

one minute after every eight lengths. Eight lengths swimming, using all the strokes alternately (including butterfly, if possible), resting for 30 seconds between each length. Eight lengths easy swimming.

During the warm-up, it is best to start off easily, building up your speed throughout the time allowed. Avoid breaststroke, and make sure that you are completely relaxed at the end of the period, ready for the hard work to follow. You should plan your own warm-up, possibly based on your main programme.

YOUR HEART RATE

A simple way to monitor improvement in your general fitness level is to check your pulse. There are two places where you can do this.

One is just below your jawbone, about 2'' (5 cm) from your ear, and the other is in the wrist (with the palm facing upwards). Count the number of beats for six seconds, and then multiply the figure by ten to find the number of beats per minute. As your fitness improves, you will find that your resting pulse rate, that is your pulse rate first

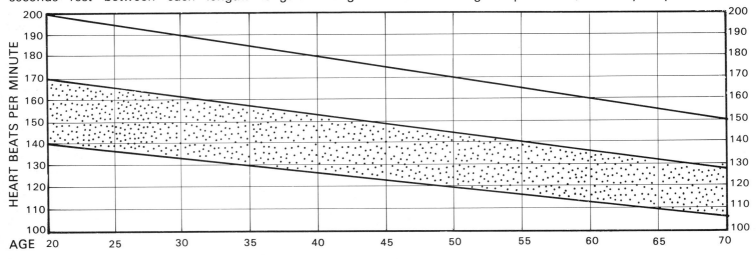

Recommended heart rates. The shaded area shows the target for your age.

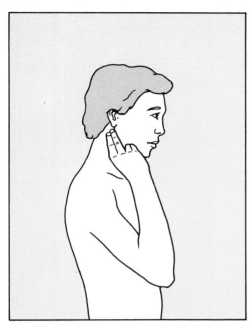

You can feel your pulse below the cheekbone.

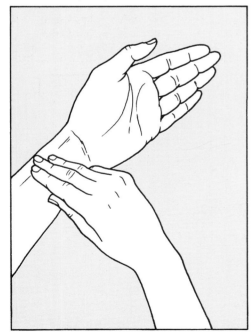

You can feel your pulse in the wrist.

thing in the morning before you get out of bed, will reduce.

During exercise you should work sufficiently hard in order to maintain your heart rate at the level recommended for your age, as shown on the chart. Take care not to exceed these recommended levels, particularly in the early stages.

You will find that when you first start exercising, it will be quite easy to raise your heart rate to the required levels. However, as your fitness improves, you may find that after exercise your heart rate is not as high as it should be, and that it recovers to your normal pulse rate more speedily. This means that you need to spend more time exercising and to work harder.

Build up to three sessions per week when your heart rate is maintained at the recommended levels for periods of up to 30 minutes. You will find that the work will become much easier after a time, not only because your fitness improves, but also because your swimming skills will improve, especially if you follow the guidelines given for the various strokes.

USEFUL HINTS

Whether you are swimming for fitness, or simply for recreation, it is a good idea to organize your visits to the pool. The following hints are for your guidance.

1. Plan in advance what you intend to do at each session, and try to stick to it. If you get tired, choose a simpler programme next time.
2. Keep a record of all your swimming sessions. This will help to ensure that your work is progressive.
3. It is always best to bring variety into your programme to make sure that your interest is maintained. Programmes can be built around swimming to improve your technique, swimming extended distances without stopping, swimming shorter distances with occa-

sional rests and trying to maintain speed, swimming legs only or swimming arms only. All these activities can be built into one session.
4. Another way to introduce variety is to use all the strokes, or as many different strokes as you can.
5. Always devote some of the period to improving your swimming style. Once again make use of the drawings in this book.
6. Start all your sessions with five minutes gentle swimming to get your circulation moving. Gradually work up to a more vigorous pace, and after your fitness session finish off with two or three minutes more gentle swimming.
7. When using the legs only drills outlined earlier in this book, always use a float held out in front of your head with the arms extended.
8. When using the arms only drills, put a float or a pull buoy between your upper legs to give support.
9. If you wish to swim lengths, you may have to wait for a quiet period at the pool. Find out if there are any special times when lane ropes are put down for this purpose.
10. When swimming distances, try not to stop at each end of the pool, but turn round immediately.
11. When swimming shorter distances, for example single lengths, try to take just enough rest to enable you to maintain your pace. On these occasions concentrate on swimming fast.
12. Learn to use a pace clock. Many pools have one. It helps you to check your swimming speed accurately and to monitor your rest periods.
13. Once you have built up a better level of fitness, it is a good idea to work out a system whereby you work reasonably hard on one visit, and then not so hard on the next visit. This method enables you to concentrate on technique during the easier sessions.

GROUP SWIMMING

Swimming can be a very good group sport. It is a sport where there are no barriers of age or physical size, and is a great leveller. It is also a true family sport where parents can enjoy fun in the water alongside their children.

FAMILY SWIMMING

It would be useful to check with your local pool to see if they have any particular evenings set aside for family swimming. This means that fairly large groups can get together to take part in games or other activities. There may also be fun nights when extra inflatable aids or other objects are put into the pool to increase swimmers' enjoyment.

It is good if a family can attend the pool regularly so that everyone can help each other. Father can help his children, and eventually the children can guide father. In some skills, it is helpful if one person can observe what you are doing, checking your technique against the picture sequences in this book. This is particularly good when diving.

If you are a parent and feel that your child has developed to a good level of swimming, you may decide that he/she needs the help and guidance of an experienced teacher. This does not mean that your job is over. It is still helpful to have family sessions in the pool where you can offer encouragement and comment to your child to keep him/her interested in developing their ability further.

It is fun for families to get involved in a simple fitness programme. A simple method is to draw up record cards for each member of the family, and to record the distance swum at each visit to the pool. You can even pin up a chart in the kitchen, and make targets for the family in the ways described on page 86. It does not mean that you all have to visit the pool at once.

WATER GAMES

There are a great many games which you can play in the water. Most of these are very simple and need little or no equipment. You can play them with quite large groups of people, and in fact you will probably find that you will invent your own games as you go along.

Simon Says is a basic adaptation of a game from the playground. One person is nominated as leader. The leader decides on an activity, and when he says Simon Says you will all dive or Simon Says you will all swim a width, everyone copies Simon. Then someone else takes over as leader. This is a particularly good game for encouraging swimmers to extend their skills.

Ring-a-Ring-a-Roses is another playground adaptation. Here a group forms into a small circle in water about shoulder-depth. Go through the ring-a-ring-a-roses nursery rhyme, and when you come to the end you all fall down, submerging under water. This is a useful game for getting swimmers accustomed to getting their faces wet. If you keep on holding hands until you resurface, this means that it is not possible to wipe the water from your face. It therefore encourages you to shake your head to remove surface water, as described on page 18.

What's the Time Mr. Wolf? is a familiar playground game. One person is nominated as the wolf, who swims in front. The others follow, chanting 'What's the time Mr. Wolf?'. The leader turns round and says the time. When he says '12 o'clock', that is the signal for the others to escape. They swim away from the wolf as quickly as possible, and the wolf tries to catch as many as he can.

Fishes is a game for a group of five or six people. The group forms a circle holding hands, with one, two or maybe three people inside the circle. The people forming the circle kick their legs vigorously, and try to make the circle to move round fast. The object is for the people inside the circle to swim out of the circle by swimming under the arms of the others. If they manage to escape, the fishes are free to swim.

Sharks is a particularly good game for large groups of around eight or nine people. One person is nominated as the shark. The others are the fishes. Everyone lines up in the water on one side of the pool. At a signal all the fishes must attempt to swim across the width of the pool to get to the other side. The job of the shark is to catch as many fishes as possible. As soon as you are caught, you change from being a fish and become a shark. This procedure is repeated until only one fish is left. This person becomes the shark for the next game.

Rats and Rabbits is another game for large groups of eight to ten people. One person is nominated as the caller, and this person remains out of the water. The others line up in the water, all on the same side of the pool. This group is then split in two halves, one of rats and one of rabbits. The caller calls out either rats or rabbits. If for instance he calls out rats, then the rats push themselves away from the side as quickly as possible, trying to swim to the other side. Meanwhile the job of the rabbits is to chase them and to catch them up before they reach the other side.

Crocodiles Here you form a line, where people hold each other around the waist and swim in a big crocodile along the pool. The object is for the person at the front to try and catch the person at the back. This game can in fact be played either swimming or else just walking in the shallow end. If you wish, you can make a variation by playing the game to music.

MORE WATER GAMES

Apart from the simple games which are adapted from the playground, there are plenty of other games such as ball games and races.

Blowing Game This is a very simple game, which is particularly popular with young swimmers. In fact you do not need to be a competent swimmer at all. You need a ping-pong ball for each person. The game is to swim across the width of the pool blowing the ball along in front of you as you go. The person who can blow it furthest is the winner. This game is helpful for developing your water breathing technique. To play it well you need to get your face very close to the water.

Obstacle Races There are many objects such as hoops, floating vertical sticks, or objects placed on the bottom of the pool, which can be used to create interesting obstacle courses. Some very simple races can be set up where it is necessary to swim in and out of vertical sticks, or to swim through hoops and then continue under water to the next hoop. You can also fetch objects from the bottom of the pool and then put them back again. All these games can be timed to see who can do them quickest.

Other Races You can perform all kinds of races, and these can be varied to make them easier or more difficult. Racing with rubber rings, racing holding a float and kicking, and racing doing any stroke or combination of strokes are just some ideas, which you can easily develop for yourself.

Diving to the Bottom is always a popular game, as it can be adapted around many objects. Throw any object that will sink into the pool, and then try to recover it, either by surface diving or by jumping in and submerging, or else by diving from the side. This can be turned into a competition where you throw a number of objects into the pool and then try to recover these one at a time, seeing who can recover the most, either until there are none left or else within a given time. A variation is to allocate for example four objects to each person, and then to paint them different colours, and to see who can recover their four objects the fastest. This is particularly good for involving a family, with father making the objects and mother painting them in pretty colours.

Strings and Pegs is a game to encourage going under water and opening your eyes under water. Here you have a line of pegs, which are clipped onto a string hanging down under water from a float. You simply go under water and gradually work down the string removing all the pegs. In order to get close to the pegs you need to feel confident under water. This game can be extended into quite deep water.

Water Basket Ball For this you have to buy a special basket ball net which floats on the water. These are available from high quality sports shops, and tend to be fairly expensive. Before making the purchase or playing the game, always check that you are allowed to play in the pool. You can play various games. You can simply take it in turns to throw a ball into the basket from a set distance, or else you can have a competitive game with two teams, one team attacking and one team defending the basket.

Simple Water Polo Water polo is a complicated game with rules and tactics, rather like ice hockey or American football. It is not practical for a family or group to play a full game, so you need to adapt it. You can pile up floats on one side of the pool, and then form two teams with one defending and one attacking, and a goalkeeper. You can make things more difficult by allowing catches with one instead of two hands, and you can outlaw submersion. Be careful, as some pools are not designed for ball games, and you must always check with the attendant. When you become more proficient you can play the game in deeper water, and also go up and down the pool, if there is room.

SYNCHRONIZED SWIMMING

This offers a new and exciting sport, particularly appealing to girls when they have mastered the skills of swimming. Many young boys enjoy practising some of the routines, but at the moment the top level competitions are restricted to girls. In order to become proficient, you need to be able to scull and to be completely happy under water for prolonged periods.

Synchronized swimming is in fact water ballet, with routines set to music. You can learn it on your own, and there are even competitions for individuals. If you find that you enjoy it, you can then join a group which allows you to take part in displays involving up to eight partners. In order to reach the highest standards, you need not only good body awareness and a sense of rhythm, but you must also be extremely fit.

COMPETITIVE SWIMMING

If you want to swim in competitions, you must be prepared to dedicate yourself to the sport. You will need to spend a considerable amount of time in training each week. Before you enter a training programme, you must be an all-round swimmer, be proficient in at least three of the four strokes, and have developed the skills of diving as described in this book.

WHAT DOES IT TAKE?

You may have wondered how the top international swimmers achieve their speed and skill. The answer is that there is a combination of factors involved. If you want to take part in competitions, you will need natural skill, strength, endurance, flexibility, and the right mental attitudes.

Some swimmers may have all these qualities, but still never achieve the highest standards. What sets an excellent swimmer apart from the average one is that 'X' factor that cannot be coached. It is simply there. It is like the difference between Charles Dickens and an ordinary writer.

If you have natural skill, a coach can adapt your technique to make the best use of this skill. You can improve your strength by a land conditioning programme, using weight training or other exercises. But remember what has been said on resistance (see page 22), and that it is important to gain strength without adding to body bulk. Endurance is best achieved by training in the water, but can be helped on land by circuit training, running or games. Your flexibility can be improved by following a systematic series of exercises.

It is important to seek the guidance of a qualified coach who can present you with an organized training programme. A good relationship with a coach is helpful in developing the right mental attitudes and motivation. Even if you only aspire to swimming well at club level, this will require considerable amounts of training each week. You must be prepared to work hard during each session, and also to put in some work on land conditioning.

YOUR FIRST COMPETITION

Since the first visit to a gala or competition is often strange and difficult, what follows below are a few notes for your guidance.

What to Take Since you will probably need to swim more than once, and it is uncomfortable to sit around in wet costumes, take extra costumes as well as a supply of towels. Dry yourself after each swim, and keep warm to prevent injury to muscles and to ensure the best performance. If necessary, wear a track suit, and even socks and training shoes while waiting for your event.

The Warm-Up is a preparation for physical activity prior to the competition, normally lasting thirty minutes, but check the time allowed. Do not over-tire yourself, but prepare yourself well for the race. A coach will help you to develop the warm-up suited to your needs. A typical procedure consists of easy stroke swimming, some drills, some fast hard swimming, checking starts and turns and finally swim down, i.e. slow easy swimming.

The Pool Layout is different for galas. The pool is divided into lanes with ropes. There are starting blocks, possibly at each end. Flags are located five metres from each end over the top of the water to help backstrokers in their turns and finishes. Also a rope is placed about half way down the pool for recalling a false start.

Knowing What to Do There is usually someone who announces the races and keeps you informed of progress. But do not rely on others to tell you when your event is coming. Keep yourself aware of the progress of the programme. Often there are stewards who organize competitors into their individual races. Introduce yourself to your steward in advance. When you have been given a lane number, wait behind the starting block for your race.

A number of short blasts on a whistle by the starter or referee means that the race is about to start. A single long blast indicates that you must take up your starting position. Always take up your position quickly. If at your first gala you do not wish to dive off a starting block, it is quite in order to dive from the side. Your position must be alongside the block, one pace back from the edge. If your diving is not up to standard, notify the starter or referee that you wish to start in the water. This is better than jumping in, which is slow. Enter the water after the single long blast. For butterfly and breaststroke, hold the wall with two hands facing the course. For frontcrawl, you only need hold the wall with one hand.

You will then hear the command 'Take Your Marks'. It is important here to concentrate on the starting signal, not the mechanics of the start. The signal will be either a gun, a whistle, the word 'Go' or even a klaxon. In the event of a false start you will hear repeated starting signals or a whistle, and the false start rope will be dropped. Return to your starting block, and the procedure will be repeated. Remember that on the third start, the starter will start the race irrespective of any infringements, and any competitor who goes early will be disqualified.

During the Race judges will observe your style to ensure that you conform with the relevant laws. Judges will also watch your turns and your finish. When you have finished, remain in the water until the referee tells you to leave. After the race, get changed immediately and keep warm.

Winning Many races are won by very small margins, and the difference between success and failure is often due to poor starting and turning. So you must perform starts and turns really well, and understand the techniques involved.

Good starts have two common features. First, a powerful push off with the legs from the poolside or starting block. This means that you must develop strong leg muscles. Second, the entry into the water must be streamlined, which means that the rest of the body should enter the water through the same hole made by the hands.

For good turns, you must approach the wall without any loss of speed. You must execute the turn as fast as possible, with a strong and vigorous drive off the wall. Finally, you must make a smooth transition from the turn to the stroke, with be no loss of momentum.

Winning is not the most important thing. Remember there can only be one winner in any race. You can have a lot of fun taking part in competitions and

from the companionship of your team mates. So don't always expect to be successful.

1. Announcer. 2. Recorders 3. Finishing Judges 4. Time Keepers 5. Backstroke Flags 6. Referee 7. False Start Rope. 8. Starter with gun 9. Style Judges 10. Competition Steward 11. Turn Judge.

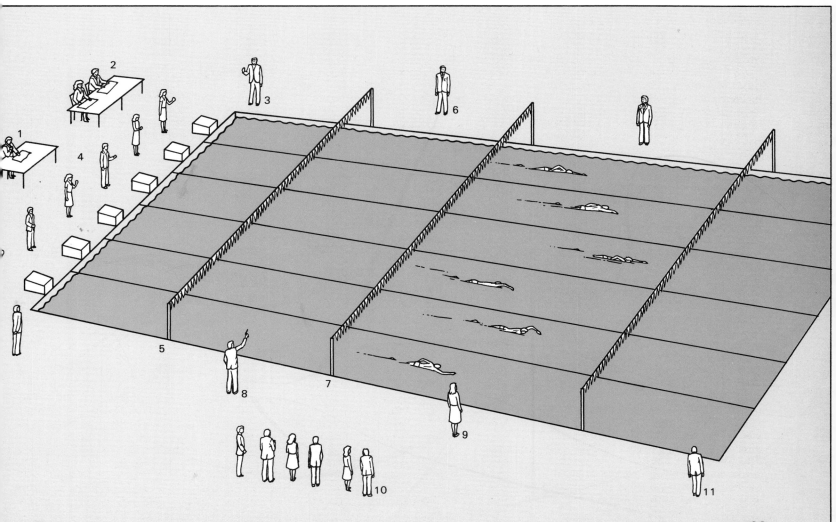

GRAB START

The Grab Start is used when you are starting a race using a start signal. It is generally agreed that this is the fastest forward racing start. Because you can make use of your hands as well as your feet to push off, it has been found that entry into the water is quicker.

Preparation Stand behind the starting block, and at the signal from the referee, mount the back of the block. Concentrate on the start only, and listen carefully for the starter's instructions. Avoid all distractions.

Take your Marks On hearing this command, step forward to the front edge of the block. Place the feet hip-width apart, curling the toes firmly over the front of the block. Then take hold of the block with your hands, either inside or outside the feet, with the arms nearly straight. To achieve this, bend the knees slightly. The position should be firm, with the hips held as far forward as possible without overbalancing.

It is important now to concentrate on the starting signal rather than the movements of the start. This will help to achieve a quick reaction, and thus a faster start, when the signal goes off.

Go! As soon as you hear the signal, pull against the front edge of the block, causing the body to overbalance. The knees drop and the legs begin to bend in readiness for a strong push off. The head should now be raised, allowing the eyes to look forward down the pool. The body continues to overbalance as you push the arms forward towards an extended position. When the knees have dropped close to the level of the feet, extend the legs vigorously, thus driving the body upward and outward off the block.

Flight When you have left the block, lower the head to produce a streamlined body shape. At this point, you can make a choice. Either you can maintain a straight body and so enter the water with a fairly flat entry, or else you can slightly bend the body at the highest point of the dive and so create a deeper entry with less resistance. This last method allows the rest of the body to enter through the same hole as the hands, while the first method is easier to perform but creates more turbulence.

Entry On Entry, the hands should be close together, fingers pointed, with the head between the arms. When the feet enter the water, the ankles should be stretched.

Glide After entering the water, you will commence the glide with the hands and arms stretched forward and upward towards the surface. You will usually be moving faster than when swimming. Stretch out and hold this streamlined position: head firmly between the arms, one hand on top of the other, stomach firm, legs close together and toes pointed. (Now turn to the **Underwater Swimming** section on page 76.)

SKILL AQUISITION

Before attempting to learn to start from a dive you must have some basic experience of diving. First of all, you must develop and practice the basic water confidence and diving skills described on pages 18 and 58. You must be capable of doing the basic Plunge Dive, which in fact leads naturally into the racing dive.

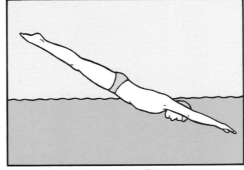

Start with a basic Plunge Dive.

Whichever dive start you decide to learn first, they all have problems, and require constant practice. It is probably easier to start with the Grab Start, and when you have achieved some proficiency with this, you can go on to develop the Wind-Up Start. Ask someone to check your basic stance. This is to make sure that you observe the detailed points of technique correctly.

Whilst the early practices can be carried out without the use of starting blocks, in order to develop the skill properly you will need to use them as often as possible. You may find that it is necessary to begin to use the starting blocks at the shallow end of the pool. However, before you attempt to dive into shallow water, you must make sure that you are skilled at diving into deep water. Starting blocks will give you the correct experience of diving from a height. Eventually, you will need someone to time the start, to give you an objective standard of performance.

PRACTICES

1. Basic Plunge Dive from the poolside.
2. The correct start position for your racing dive.
3. Practise your chosen racing dive from the poolside.
4. Practise your racing dive from starting block.

COMMON FAULTS

Many of the faults connected with dives come from taking up a bad starting position. It is essential to maintain a good stance. Points of technique you should remember are that the feet must be placed correctly, hip-width apart, with the toes well over the edge of the pool and the hands gripping the sides securely. The head should look forward and down. You will need to monitor your position constantly to check that you are observing all these points. Ask someone to watch what you are doing.

A fault particularly associated with

the Grab Start is not pulling hard enough on the block to initiate the start. Many swimmers simply fall forward. Practice the pull repeatedly.

When divers enter the water, the fault is often a flat Entry. This will occur if you do not spot the correct entry position, which ensures that the hands enter the water first followed by the rest of the body, and with the feet entering last. Again, ask someone to observe your Flight and Entry so that you achieve the correct mechanics.

Do not forget to use the initial glide to maximum effect. This is because it is quicker than swimming. Concentrate on making the transition from this glide to the swimming stroke as smooth as possible (see page 76).

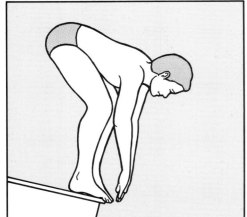

Not pulling hard enough on the block.

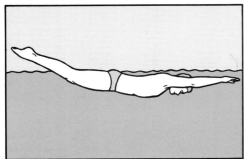

Entry too flat.

Take Your Marks.

Go!

Arms swing forward.

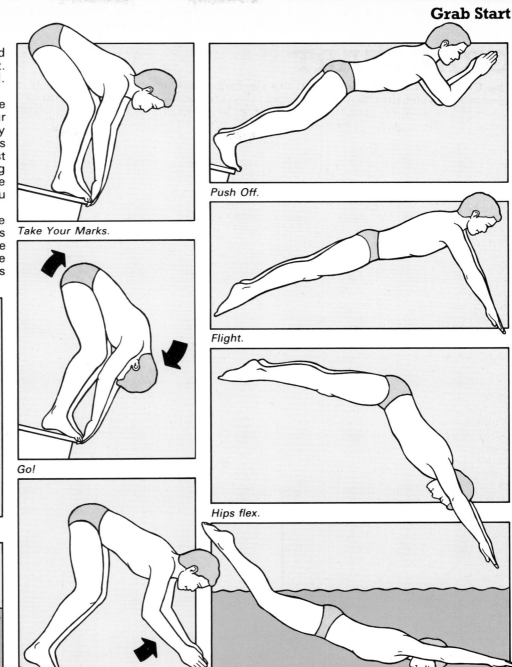

Push Off.

Flight.

Hips flex.

Entry.

WIND-UP START

If you are taking part in relay races you will need to learn this start, which is the fastest one for relay takeovers. By employing a circling movement with the arms, you can build up a large angular momentum, which when stopped can be transferred to the body to increase the acceleration from the starting block. As this fast arm action can start as the swimmer approaches the takeover point, it makes for a very fast takeover.

Preparation Stand behind the starting block, concentrating on your task in the relay. As the preceeding swimmer in the relay team turns for his last length, mount the back of the block. When the other swimmer is within his last 80 feet (20 metres) of the takeover point, you should move up to the edge of the block in a position for the takeover.

Starting Position Take up a position at the front of the block, placing your feet hip width apart, and curling the toes firmly around the front edge. Then bend forward at the trunk with slight flexion of the knees, with the arms pointing down towards the pool and the hands just outside the legs. The palms of the hands should face backwards. Concentrate now on your approaching team mate. As the swimmer enters the last 5 yards (5 metres) and approaches the wall, you should begin your start to ensure that you leave the block as soon as the swimmer touches the wall.

The Start Begins Your first action is to move the arms upwards, outwards and forwards, with the head dropping slightly. This will cause the knees to move forward of the ankles as the centre of gravity moves away from the starting block.

You should consciously build up the speed of this forward, upward and outward movement of the arms by using a slight flexion of the elbow. The arm swing continues up and round, moving backwards to form a complete circular movement. As the hands pass the shoulders, begin to lift the head. The hands continue backwards, the head continues to rise.

As the hand passes the thighs, completing the circular movement forward, begin to extend the knees to drive forward into the pool. At this point, your palms should face towards the legs, with the hands continuing to accelerate forward. A fast continuous action here is essential to ensure a good start. At no stage should there be any pause. Continue the strong drive from the block as your hands move forward to the entry position.

Push Off As the hands reach extension in front of the body, stop the circular arm action. Hold the head steady, look forward and down into the pool. The tremendous momentum developed by the arm action and head movement is now transferred to your body, and will assist with the strong push off the block. Extend your feet vigorously as they leave the block. At this point, you must spot your entry position and lowr your head in line with the arms to ensure a clean entry.

Entry The fingers should enter first, with the hands close together. This is similar to the Entry for the grab start. The rest of the body follows through the same point in the water, and tension should be maintained throughout the body until the toes are submerged.

SKILL ACQUISITION

As with most diving skills, it is helpful if someone can observe what you are doing and give you guidance. This start, with its somewhat complicated build-up, requires regular practice, particularly to ensure that the arm movements are timed correctly with the leg movements. In the later stages, you should practice relay takeovers, with a swimmer in the water pretending to finish an actual race.

Practice relay takeovers.

COMMON FAULTS

The major fault tends to be that the diver does not complete the movements properly. Do not hurry, but make sure that you make effective use of the arm movements. Do not push off the block too early in the arm action.

Pushing off too soon: feet enter before hands.

Excessive flexing of the back during Flight can be a problem. If you push off too soon, the legs may enter the water before the arms. Other faults to guard against are head out of line with the arms, the arms apart at Entry, legs bent at Entry, and legs apart at Entry.

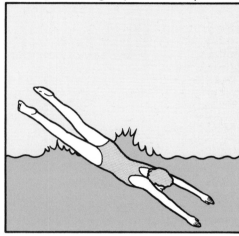

Arms and legs apart at Entry.

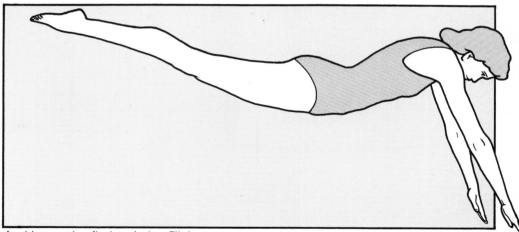

Avoid excessive flexing during Flight.

BACKCRAWL START

The Backcrawl Start is the only start where you are required to start in the water. It is a simple skill, quickly learnt by the novice. The key features to develop are a strong drive off the wall, coupled with a smooth transition from the start to swimming backcrawl.

Preparation Wait at the side of the pool behind the starting block for a signal from the referee. When the signal is given, enter the pool by any method, and quickly take up your position ready for the start.

Starting Position Grasp the backcrawl bar on the starting block if there is one, otherwise use any other grip. Face the end of the course and make no attempt to look sideways. Keep the feet in a comfortable position under the surface. If one foot is slightly higher than the other, this helps to ensure a strong, firm drive away from the wall. There should be no tension at this stage. Concentrate on the starter's instructions, and not on the movements and actions of the start.

Take your Marks On hearing this command from the starter, pull yourself into a crouched position, with the head tucked well down, looking towards the wall, and with the elbows flexed. Concentrate only on listening for the starting signal. This action can be compared to that of compressing a spring.

Go! As soon as you hear the signal, pull on the bar and push your feet against the wall to raise your body and bring your behind clear of the water. Throw your head up and back and push off from the start point with the arms upwards.

After pushing away from the wall, the arms should continue upwards and outwards with slight flexion of the elbows in an accelerating movement, until they are extended beyond the head with the arms straight. The movement of the arms is important to ensure a smooth start.

Flight You should try to move over the water, consciously arching the back and keeping the legs extended. Ideally, the whole body should rise out of the water before Entry. This usually only occurs with swimmers who have very strong leg drives.

Entry If the body has been successfully lifted out of the water, the hands should enter the water first, with the rest of the body following through the same hole. Try to arch your back to achieve this, and avoid the legs and feet entering the water before the hands.

Glide After Entry, the hands should remain extended and stretched, with one hand on top of the other, and the head in line with the trunk between the arms, and the feet extended. As the speed of the glide decreases and nears swimming speed, a smooth transition into backcrawl should occur.

Starting to Swim Establish a strong leg kick first. After four or five kicks, move one hand from the extended position and press on the water in a full movement. Keep the other hand extended above the head. As the first hand completes its propulsive movement, the second hand begins to make a full movement, which allows a smooth and continues stroke to begin.

By this stage, the body should be up at surface level ready to start the race.

SKILL ACQUISITION
This relatively simple skill merely requires regular practice. Ask someone to observe and correct your technique.

PRACTICES
1. The basic start on its own followed by a glide.
2. Carry out a push glide and practice a smooth transition to swimming. Concentrate on starting with the leg kick followed by the hand movement.
3. Practise the whole skill.

COMMON FAULTS
Many people do not push off hard enough from the wall. Practice constantly to achieve this strong drive. Another fault is that the arms rise vertically rather than out and round.

Avoid the fault of pushing through the water rather than up and over it. Make sure here that the push off is hard and vigorous, and that it is upwards as well as out. Too short a glide and not making use of the speed of the start is a further fault. Ask someone to watch this, and to help you with better timing.

Avoid this fault: arms rising vertically rather than out and round.

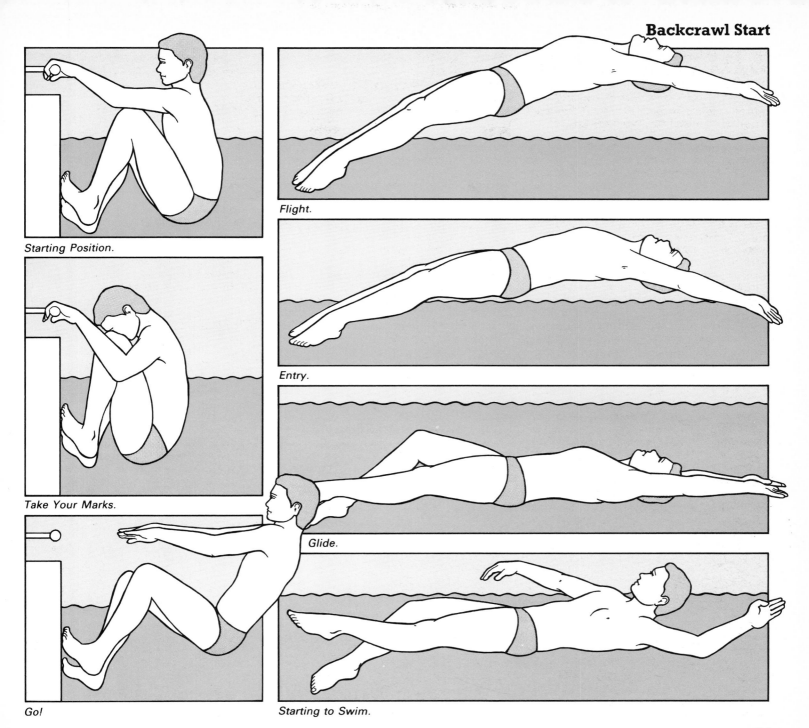

Backcrawl Start

Starting Position.

Take Your Marks.

Go!

Flight.

Entry.

Glide.

Starting to Swim.

99

FRONTCRAWL TURN

The faster and most effective turn used in frontcrawl swimming today is known as the Tumble Turn, which allows the feet to touch the wall.

The Approach As you approach the wall, observe carefully the markings on the pool floor. Normally, the central black line just before the wall finishes with a 'T'. Once you spot the approach of the T, begin to move smoothly into the turn. Leave one hand by your side, while you complete the arm pull with the other. Once both hands are beside the thigh, you are ready to start the actual turn.

The Somersault Start the somersault with a short butterfly type kick, drop the head below the surface, and press strongly down towards the bottom of the pool with the palms of your hands. As soon as your trunk begins to move downwards with flexion of the body at the hips, tuck up the legs so that they pass directly over your head over the surface of the water. Make sure that the head drives down as quickly as possible. This will help to make the turn as fast as possible. As the legs pass over head, body flexion will increase. The head will move forwards under the water in the new direction while the legs reach out until the feet make contact with the wall. You can improve the speed of this action by sculling with the hands towards the head.

The Push Off Place the feet firmly on the wall, with the knees flexed at around 130°, the head between the arms and the arms slightly flexed, ready for a strong drive off. Make sure there is no delay, and concentrate on a strong and vigorous extension of the legs. At the same time extend to a streamlined position, with the head in line with the arms. Then twist onto your front at a depth of 10–12″ (25–30 cm) below the surface. For maximum streamlining, rest one hand on top of the other. As you leave the wall, hold the streamlined position until the glide slows down. As soon as you sense the speed falling,

transfer smoothly to swimming.

Starting to Swim First establish a strong leg kick. After two or three kicks, the bottom hand should begin to press out and down into the stroke. This helps the body to rise to the surface. Do not try to lift the head during this action.

SKILL ACQUISITION

You may find it quite difficult to learn tumble turning if you are not naturally gymnastic. Essentially the skill stems from a simple somersault. This is something you can learn early on in your swimming development. You need to be entirely happy with submerging the face. So you may want to revert to the basic water confidence practices (see pages 18 and 58). The somersaulting skill requires the use of the head to initiate the movement. The knees need to tuck up tight into the chest, and the hands must be used in a sculling action to speed up the somersault movement.

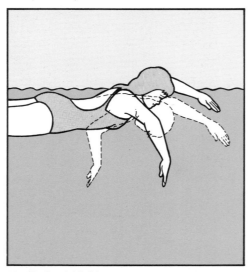

Head should initiate movement.

In order to develop the technique of the turn itself you must learn to swim frontcrawl well and to transfer smoothly into a forward somersault. This smooth transition is an important ingredient in the performance of the turn. After this you can move on to learning to carry out this action close to the wall, pushing off initially onto the back, and swimming away using backcrawl. Finally, you can develop the full turn, pushing off onto the front.

Once these basic elements have been learnt, you will need to practice constantly to speed up the turning process and to ensure a really smooth transition from swimming to turn, and from turn to swimming. At some stage, it will be necessary to ask someone to time you to give you an objective standard for developing further.

PRACTICES
1. Basic water confidence work for submerging under water.
2. A forward somersault from standing position.
3. Swim frontcrawl and transfer to a somersault.
4. Swim frontcrawl, somersault by the wall, push off and swim backcrawl.
5. Swim frontcrawl, perform the turn in full and push off slowly onto the front.
6. As (5) above, but speed up the process.

COMMON FAULTS
On the Approach, the main fault is loss of speed due to the head being lifted prior to initiating the turn. You must remember to keep the head low at this point, and concentrate on making a smooth transition from swimming to turn.

During the turn, do not let the hips drop. Keep the legs together and clear of the water. Often turns appear untidy because the legs are apart and bent. This leads to slower turning, and should

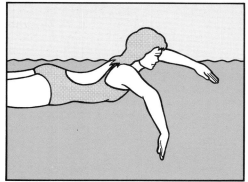

Do not lift head before the turn.

Avoid untidy leg actions.

be avoided at all costs. The legs must move swiftly across the surface of the water towards the wall.

On the Push Off, the main fault is not pushing strongly and firmly enough. Swimmers also tend to push off on the surface rather than under water. Another fault is not making effective use of the underwater glide. A strong, firm glide is an essential ingredient in the frontcrawl turn.

THE LAW

You must remember when you are performing the tumble turn that your hand will not have touched the wall. Therefore your feet must make contact with it during the turn.

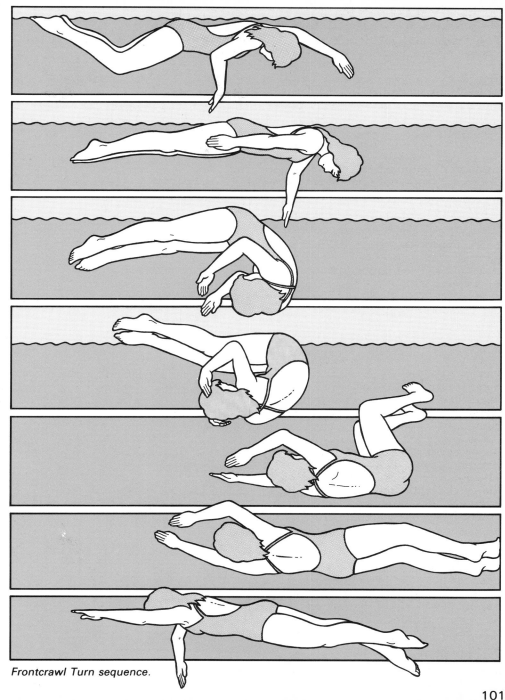

Frontcrawl Turn sequence.

BACKCRAWL TURN

Most competitive swimmers use the Spin Turn in backcrawl. It has proved to be not only the easiest to master, but also the quickest to perform.

The Approach The problem with backstroke swimming is that we cannot use the pool floor marking. Flags have to be provided 5 yards (5 metres) from the turning or finishing end. Practice your turning technique with the flags in position so that you learn to approach the wall correctly. The competent swimmer should be able to judge his approach without looking for the turning end. But the novice may need to check positions just before the turn. Do so by dropping and rotating your head to look over the shoulder of your leading arm as your hand enters the water.

The Touch A touch must be made before going into the turn. Use the hand if possible, although the Law also allows a touch with the leading arm or the head. Do not leave your back until a touch is made. As the last stroke is completed, drop your head back and recover the arm over your face to make contact with the wall directly behind your head, about 12" (30 cm) below the surface. The position of the touch is important, as the turn beings from this point. The fingers should point down and out towards the opposite shoulder to give a firm position from which to start the spin.

The Spin As soon as you have made the touch, the arm begins to flex and then extends quickly to initiate spin. Flex the legs and lift them clear of the water, keeping the feet and knees together. To spin faster, use the free arm to scull towards the top of the head, while the legs are thrown round towards the wall.

If you touch with the right hand, you must swing the legs towards the right shoulder. Similarly, a left hand touch calls for a left-handed spin. At the end of the spin, the feet should be where the hands touched the wall. The hand should have left the wall and pushed through to beyond the head, although not quite extended.

The Push Off For maximum glide effect, the strong push off must occur under water. Extend the arms fully, with one hand resting on top of the other for good streamlining, and the head between the arms.

Starting to Swim As the speed of the glide decreases, start a strong leg kick. After two or three kicks, the bottom hand should press on the water in the normal way. This will lift you to the surface. Any attempt to lift the head will cause loss of streamlining and speed.

SKILL ACQUISITION

In many ways, the problems facing the development of the backcrawl turn are similar to those of the frontcrawl turn. Once again, go back to basic water confidence work before you start to learn the turn.

The basic movements of the spin are very simple. It can be helpful if you lie on the water, tuck up your legs towards the chest and just practice the skill of sculling around in a circle. This will give you the feel of the correct position. You can then go on to develop the turn by swimming to the wall and starting this movement from the wall.

PRACTICES

1. Basic water confidence work for submerging under water.
2. Scull on the back.
3. Scull in a tucked position on your back.
4. Swim slowly to the wall and perform the turn.
5. Speed up the whole process.

COMMON FAULTS

On the Approach, many swimmers look too often for the pool end. You must learn to use the backstroke flags when learning the turn. Otherwise you will always destroy the body position while you are checking for the end.

Lie on the water and tuck up the legs to get used to the spin.

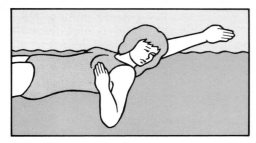

Do not look for the pool end.

During the turn, untidy actions will have a slowing-down effect. To avoid these, make sure that the feet and knees come clear of the water, and move round smoothly to the wall.

Avoid untidy actions.

On the Push Off, a common fault is to push off on the surface of the water instead of making effective use of the glide. To develop this basic skill, you should practice pushing and gliding under water with a smooth transition to the swimming stroke.

THE LAW

You must make the touch before you leave your back for the turn. You can touch with the hand or leading arm, shoulder or head. You must be on your back before your feet lose contact with the wall after the turn, and you must remain on your back throughout the race.

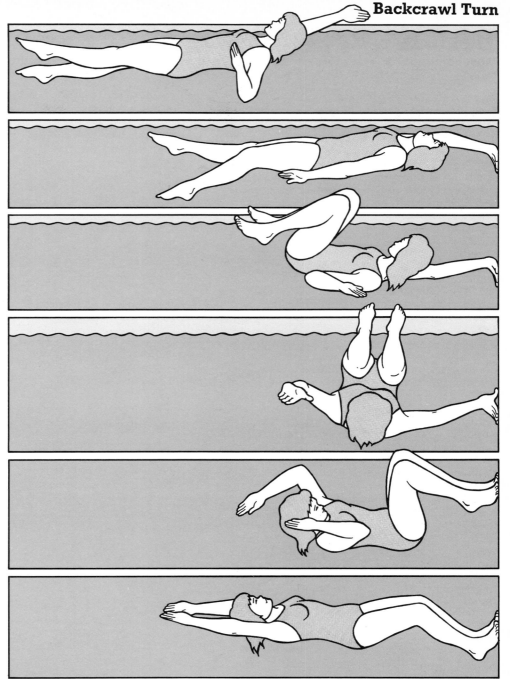

Backcrawl Turn sequence.

BREASTSTROKE AND BUTTERFLY TURNS

The rules governing the Breaststroke Turn are somewhat different to those for the other turns. A competitive swimmer is allowed to take one stroke of the arms and legs under water before surfacing. The novice need not attempt this in the early stages, and can just surface and start swimming in the normal way. But it is recommended that you learn to do it, as it is much faster to swim under water than on the surface.

The Approach The Law requires that you touch the end of the pool with two hands simultaneously. So continue to swim the stroke strongly towards the wall. Aim to touch it with the arms fully extended, taking care not to allow your head to go beneath the surface. As soon as the touch is made, your speed should allow the arms to flex, and you can pull yourself in towards the wall, lifting the head quickly. This action will cause the legs and trunk to drop in the water, and thus to effect the turn.

The Turn To ensure the quickest possible turn, the hips and knees should flex under water. Aim to get round quickly and to go back up the pool on the same line as you approached.

One hand leaves the wall fast, and moves down towards the ribs, palms up, as the body rotates. The other arm pushes away from the wall, and moves over the surface to slice into the water, and the head follows. This action allows the feet to move round to fix firmly on the wall, facing back down the pool.

The Push Off With the body 12–15'' (30–37 cm) below the surface, and the arms extended, drive strongly off the wall. Hold the hands with thumbs together, pitched out and ready to swim. Hold the head in a normal position between the arms, and the legs together and extended.

The First Arm Pull As the speed of the first glide slows down, pull backwards with a long arm stroke through to the thighs, similar to doing butterfly stroke. This strong pull will accelerate the body

speed, and allow a second glide to take place, while the hands are still held close to the thighs. Hold the head in a normal position, and do not attempt to lift it yet.

The Kick As the second glide slows down, push the hands and arms forwards close to the body under the chest. Keep the elbows well in, while the feet also recover and kick back strongly. Timing is crucial here. The kick should be complete as the arms reach the extended position. The head should break the surface at the same time.

Starting to Swim If the timing of the underwater swimming is correct, you should find that as you have completed the kick the arms are extended and the head has broken the surface. You can now move smoothly into the normal breaststroke rhythm.

BUTTERFLY TURN

As with breaststroke, the touch must be made with two hands. Thereafter, the mechanics of the turn are the same. However, there is no underwater phase as such, but the strong push off from the wall is essential, with the feet starting the kick after the glide, followed by the arm movement. Novices finding themselves short of the wall on approach should kick in hard to the wall, keeping the arms extended. Do not attempt an extra stroke. The transition to swimming will be earlier in butterfly, as this is a faster stroke.

SKILL ACQUISITION

The basic elements of the initial part of the breaststroke and butterfly turns are very similar. Therefore they can be practised together. In fact the movements are so simple that little instruction is needed to develop the skill at the beginning. All you need to do is to practice regularly, and to learn to speed up the whole process. Concentrate first on the Touch and Push Off. These must be properly developed before you attempt to practice the underwater phase of the breaststroke action, as this requires careful attention.

It is difficult to break down the skill as a learning process other than suggest that you practise approaching the wall in order to gain the correct approach, speed and position. You can then develop the Approach together with the Turn, and finally incorporate the strong drive off.

The underwater phase of breaststroke is the only problem, because the timing is difficult. You need to make sure that once you have carried out the one underwater stroke, the head has broken the surface, and is clear to start swimming the stroke without any pause. This requires constant practice.

PRACTICES

1. Approach the wall with the correct touch.
2. Approach the wall, transfer to turn with push and glide.
3. Push and glide with underwater breaststroke action.
4. Touch, turn, push and glide, and follow with underwater phase of breaststroke.
5. Speed up the process, possibly with timing.

COMMON FAULTS

On the Approach, many swimmers slow down too much, and also fail to make the touch at arm's length. This touch is important for a strong turn. Learn to gauge your approach accurately so that you touch the end of the pool at arm's length and in the correct manner. Another problem is to get too close to the wall when performing the turn, which makes the movement difficult.

The creation of a lot of splash merely wastes energy. During the turn, you must develop a strong swift action with the knees well bent under the body. Strong use of the hands and head ensures speed of movement.

Many of the faults associated with the Push Off are similar to those for the other turns: an ineffective drive off from the wall, not making full use of the underwater glide phase, and pushing off on the surface. The underwater drive and the maintenance of a streamlined body position are both very important.

There are a few special problems connected with the breaststroke action. One fault is not holding the second glide after the long arm pull through the thighs. Another is recovering away from the body rather than in a close stream-lined manner close to the body. Finally, do not pause after the leg kick whilst the head surfaces. You will find that these faults can only be corrected by constant practice.

THE LAW

For breaststroke turns the law is very strict. The touch must be made with both hands simultaneously and the shoulders must be parallel with the surface of the water. The touch may be made on, above or below the surface of the water. Whilst it is permissible at the turn for the hands to be slightly out of line with one hand higher than the other, at the finish they must be in line. With this in mind, it is best to make the touch with the hands in line at all times. After the touch, you may move off the breast for the purpose of turning. But before the feet lose contact with the wall for the strong push off, you must have returned to the breast and be parallel with the surface of the water

again. You are then permitted one complete stroke under water before surfacing.

The law for butterfly is similar to that for breaststroke. The touch must be made with both hands simultaneously. Mis-alignment of the hands is not per-mitted. The shoulders must be parallel with the surface, and you must have returned to the breast and be parallel with the surface before the feet leave the wall. The turn may be made by touching the wall on, above or below the surface.

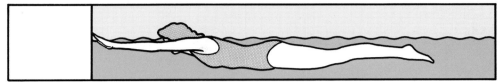

The Touch.

Knees flex, head lifts.

Drop into the water.

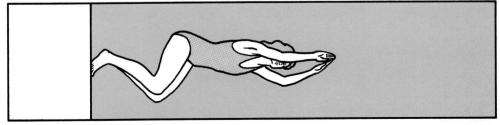

Push off strongly.

INDEX

AUTHOR'S ACKNOWLEDGEMENTS

I should like to thank members of the Droitwich Dolphins Swimming Club for the encouragement that they have given me over the years, and for their help in developing my knowledge of swimming, both from the practical standpoint of working with the club, and also for their continual encouragement to seek wider knowledge.

I am grateful to all the people who have come on courses which I have tutored. I have often found that information flows in both directions, and I have thus gained as much as the candidates have. This book includes many of the ideas which have come out of these courses.

I should like to thank Joe Dixon whose excellent photographs helped to clarify the illustrations for the Starts and Turns section. Also all the members of Amersham Swimming Club who helped with reference material for the illustrations. Other people I wish to thank are Jill Wilding for her help on the water games, and Julie and Sue for their patience in typing the text.

The water exercises on pages 82–5 are adapted from E. Bolton and D. Goodwin: **Introduction to Pool Exercises** published by E & S. Livingstone, 1956.

EDITOR'S ACKNOWLEDGEMENTS

Imogen Bright would like to thank all the people who have helped to contribute to this book, particularly everyone who has helped on the major task of producing the illustrations. First of all the illustrators themselves:

Peter Menim
Kate Simunek
Steve Wheldon

who have worked extremely hard. Secondly, Joe Dixon for all his support, his help on the Starts and Turns as well as the cover photographs.

I am also very grateful to everyone at Amersham Swimming Club who helped with putting together the reference: Chris Hirst for his interest, advice and encouragement; Andrew Moore for posing for the cover and the Wind-Up Start sequence; Vanessa Bagot also for posing for the cover; Maura Burne and David and Alexander for help with the Basic Skills section; Joanna Dyas and Jonathan for their expertise on the Diving section; Kelvin Grimwood for posing for the Aids spread; finally Lesley Bailey with Steve Martin, Anna Head, Nadine Newton, Jan Digby, Susan Head and Fiona Ashley for their help on the Rescues and Resuscitation spreads. Also Tony Simons for his work with the early photography, and Helen for posing for some of the strokes.